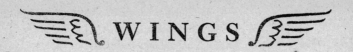

WINGS

An Anthology of Flight

edited by

H. G. BRYDEN

FABER AND FABER LIMITED

24 Russell Square

London

First published in Mcmxlii
by Faber and Faber Limited
24 Russell Square London W.C.1
R. MacLehose and Company Limited
The University Press Glasgow

PREFACE

Standing on the seashore on a late autumn day, watching the sanderlings like silver petals flashing rhythmically over the deep blue sea, following the graceful glide of a gull, or gazing at the magical illusion of black and white as a flock of lapwings swirls backwards and forwards with a lightning turn over a grey-green field, can one wonder that throughout the ages, man has longed to fly even as the birds?

Denied wings by the Creator, he has grappled with the problem of flight. Leonardo da Vinci once said 'The Lord dost sell all good things unto us at the price of labour', and so, at last, rewarded for all his passionate striving, man flies.

Along with the intense desire to fly, there always persisted in men's minds, a dread of the use to which that power, once gained, might be put—a dread proved only too well founded in our day.

Nearly three centuries ago, da Lana, in his 'Prodromo', drew as true a picture of our bombed world as if it were written to-day.

But in the welter of destruction around us, we must not forget the constructive uses to which the aeroplane will once again contribute in the days of peace. Recently the Under-Secretary of State for Air reminded the members of the Air Defence Cadet Corps that they might be 'the pilots of the New Age when one of man's greatest inventions will be used, not for his destruction but for his good, his enlightenment and his prosperity'.

And what of the enrichment of life through the joy of flight, the wider vision of the splendour of the skies and the sense of new-found power which the airman knows?

These are some of the thoughts I have tried to trace through the ages in this Anthology of Flight.

H. G. B.

CONTENTS

Contents

Contents

Contents

Contents

Contents

Contents

X. PERIL AND PRAYER

XI. WAR

Contents

Contents

The whole spirit of the World is changing and its problems are new—Speed is the dominant keynote of life—speed and energy. A new Calling has come into being, which is really the spirit of the old pioneers aflame in a new form—transport by air, the uninterrupted navigable ocean that comes to the threshold of every man's door.

First over Everest

I
Flight in Legend and Myth

WINGS IN HEAVEN

I saw the LORD sitting upon a throne, high and lifted up and his train filled the temple.

Above it stood the seraphims:

Each one had six wings; with twain he covered his face, and with twain he covered his feet, and with twain he did fly.

And one cried unto another, and said, Holy, holy, holy, is the Lord of hosts: the whole earth is full of his glory.

ISAIAH

THE VISION OF EZEKIEL

And I looked, and behold, a whirlwind came out of the north, a great cloud, and a fire infolding itself, and a brightness was about it, and out of the midst thereof as the colour of amber, out of the midst of the fire.

Also out of the midst thereof came the likeness of four living creatures. And this was their appearance; they had the likeness of a man.

And every one had four faces, and every one had four wings.

And their feet were straight feet; and the sole of their feet was like the sole of a calf's foot: and they sparkled like the colour of burnished brass.

And they had the hands of a man under their wings on their four sides; and they four had their faces and their wings.

Their wings were joined one to another; they turned not when they went; they went every one straight forward.

As for the likeness of their faces, they four had the face of a man, and the face of a lion, on the right side: and they four had the face of an ox on the left side; they four also had the face of an eagle.

Thus were their faces: and their wings were stretched upward; two wings of every one were joined one to another, and two covered their bodies.

And they went every one straight forward: whither the spirit was to go, they went; and they turned not when they went.

As for the likeness of the living creatures, their appearance was like burning coals of fire, and like the appearance of lamps: it went up and down among the living creatures; and the fire was bright, and out of the fire went forth lightning.

And the living creatures ran and returned as the appearance of a flash of lightning.

And when the living creatures went, the wheels went by them: and when the living creatures were lifted up from the earth, the wheels were lifted up.

Whithersoever the spirit was to go, they went, thither was their spirit to go; and the wheels were lifted up over against them: for the spirit of the living creature was in the wheels.

When those went, these went; and when those stood, these stood; and when those were lifted up from the earth, the wheels were lifted up over against them: for the spirit of the living creature was in the wheels.

And the likeness of the firmament upon the heads of the living creature was as the colour of the terrible crystal, stretched forth over their heads above.

And under the firmament were their wings straight, the one toward the other: every one had two, which covered on this side, and every one had two, which covered on that side, their bodies.

And when they went, I heard the noise of their wings, like the noise of great waters, as the voice of the Almighty, the voice of speech, as the noise of an host: when they stood, they let down their wings.

And there was a voice from the firmament that was over their heads, when they stood, and had let down their wings.

Ezekiel

THE ANGEL GABRIEL

Of silver wings he took a shining pair,
Fringed with gold, unwearied, nimble, swift;
With these he parts the winds, the clouds, the air,
And over seas and earth himself doth lift.
Thus clad, he cuts the spheres and circles fair,
And the pure skies with sacred feathers clift:
On Lebanon at first his foot he set
And shook his wings with rory May-dews wet.

Tasso—Translated by Ed. Fairfax
and J. Wiffan, 1600

THE FLIGHT OF RAPHAEL

(from *Paradise Lost*)

So spake the Eternal Father, and fulfilled
All justice. Nor delayed the wingèd Saint
After his charge received; but from among
Thousand celestial Ardours, where he stood
Veiled with his gorgeous wings, upspringing light,
Flew through the midst of Heaven. The angelic quires,
On each hand parting, to his speed gave way
Through all the empyreal road, till, at the gate
Of Heaven arrived, the gate self-opened wide,
On golden hinges turning, as by work
Divine the sovran Architect had framed
From hence—no cloud or, to obstruct his sight,
Star interposed, however small—he sees,
Not unconform to other shining globes,
Earth, and the Garden of God, with cedars crowned
Above all hills; as when by night the glass
Of Galileo, less assured, observes

Imagined lands and regions in the moon;
Or pilot from amidst the Cyclades
Delos or Samos first appearing kens,
A cloudy spot. Down thither prone in flight
He speeds, and through the vast ethereal sky
Sails between worlds and worlds, with steady wing
Now on the polar winds; then with quick fan
Winnows the buxom air, till, within soar
Of towering eagles, to all the fowls he seems
A phoenix—gazed by all, as that sole bird,
When, to enshrine his reliques in the Sun's
Bright temple, to Egyptian Thebes he flies.
At once on the eastern cliff of Paradise
He lights, and to his proper shape returns,
A Seraph winged. Six wings he wore, to shade
His lineaments divine: the pair that clad
Each shoulder broad came mantling o'er his breast
With regal ornament; the middle pair
Girt like a starry zone his waist, and round
Skirted his loins and thighs with downy gold
And colours dipt in Heaven; the third his feet
Shadowed from either heel with feathered mail,
Sky-tinctured grain. Like Maia's son he stood,
And shook his plumes, that heavenly fragrance filled
The circuit wide.

JOHN MILTON

THE FIRST AIRMAN

ICARUS

Give me the wings, magician! I will know
What blooms on airy precipices grow
That no hand plucks, large unexpected blossoms,
Scentless, with cry of curlews in their bosoms,
And the great winds like grasses where their stems

Spangle the universe with diadems.
I will pluck those flowers and those grasses, I,
Icarus, drowning upwards through the sky
With air that closes underneath my feet
As water above the diver. I will meet
Life with the dawn in heaven, and my fingers
Dipped in the golden floss of hair that lingers
Across the unveiled spaces and makes them colder,
As a woman's hair across her naked shoulder.
Death with the powdered stars will walk and pass
Like a man's breath upon a looking-glass,
For a suspended heart-beat making dim
Heaven brighter afterwards because of him.

Give me the wings, magician! So their tune
Mix with the silver trumpets of the moon,
And, beyond music mounting, clean outrun
The golden diapason of the sun.
There is a secret that the birds are learning
Where the long lanes in heaven have a turning
And no man yet has followed; therefore these
Laugh hauntingly across our usual seas.
I'll not be mocked by curlews in the sky;
Give me the wings, magician or I die.

His call for wings or death was heard, and thus
Came both to the first airman, Icarus.

HUMBERT WOLFE—*Personalities Early Poems*, 1930

DAEDALUS

So life went by and Daedalus was old.

There was an opening where the dizzy cliff
Made its own prison wall, and there the maze

Looked for a moment on the alien sun
Ere plunging into gloom. In that bright space
The two would sit, the boy with curious eyes
Watching the birds, till their unfettered wings
Brought to his mind new sorrow for the world
Forgotten since his childhood. Daedalus
Watched also, and looked out across the sea
Longing in heart for far-off hills and shores.
Then a thought came to him. He set the boy
To catch the wheeling gulls, and set strong snares
For every bird that came there. So for months
Of anxious toil and trial, half afraid
To hope for what might be, he fashioned wings
Of spreading perfect plumes, each feather set
In sockets of white wax: wider were they
Than those sheer pinions which Pegasus
Spread to the wind, when on Parnassus' slopes
Bellerophon first snared him at the spring;
And fairer than the wings of Zephyrus
That carried sleeping Psyche to her lord.
Then on the shoulders smooth of Icarus
He fitted them, and bound them on his arms.
Vast in the sun they spread, and dazzling,
With snowy plumes of gulls, and rainbow dyes
Of stranger birds, and golden feathers torn
From eagles of the cliff, in changeful show
On one great wing displayed. And Daedalus
Bound on himself wings duller but as wide.
Then from the steep wall of the labyrinth
Venturing they plunged downward, and the wind
Caught in the wings and arched them, till they flew
Steadily through the levels of the air.
Scarce heeded Daedalus his new-found power,
Straining his eyes in search of distant shores,

But Icarus, with his first strange freedom wild,
Joyfully tried his strength and outward soared
And upward, veering with the eddying breeze,
As the spring swallows turn and sweep and cross
In very joy. And then some wheeling bird
Caught his eye, gliding higher, and he matched
His own against its tireless wings, and sought
The spaces far above.

        There all the gods
Save those of seas and shades their dwelling have,
Untroubled by the wind or swirling storm,
By snows or burning skies or winter's chill.
They are the deathless ones, that know no change,
No sorrow or old age; for love alone
Has power upon them, and love's daughter, Joy.
Eternal and unfaltering they hold
Their peaks and palaces, from Titans won
In times forgotten of Time. Below them lie
All stars that pale at dawn before the sun,
Each ringed with leagues of silver sky; and there
Brightest of all the gods, great Phoebus shines
In light serene and pure; and still below
The clouds like islands lie above the sea.
The golden god looked on him from his throne
And wondered at his pride, who unafraid
Came where none ventured save the messenger
Of Jove, quick Mercury; with one bright ray,
Warning, he filled his eyes, while far below
Daedalus in fear cried out to him; who knows
What power, of old things mindful, filled his heart
With lust to soar? For still he forced his wings
Undaunted towards that brightness, till the god
In anger turned on the fantastic plumes
The fulness of his strength. And first, unseen,

One slipped from the expanse, and then like snow
A hundred drifted down. Too late, too late
He strove in terror towards the sheltering clouds;
As Perdix fell, he fell; and Daedalus saw
Again the anguish of despairing eyes,
More wide in terror since they fell to doom
From new-found life, and long-wished liberty.
Then on the gods he cried in bitterness
And memory swift; a moment those false wings
Stayed on the sea his son, and then the waves
Lay featherstrewn and blue. For life a life,
No more, no less, in justice they demand,
Watchers of men, the unforgetting gods.

J. LAUGHTON FIELDING—Newdigate Prize Poem, 1930

Oh! might I travel through yon lucid road,
Where rolls the chariot of the fiery God;
Might I through th' impassive air
My unwearied course pursue!
Till, distinguished from afar,
My dear country rose to view:
Then quick descending from my airy height,
My pinions would I close, and stay my flight.

EURIPIDES—*Iphigenia*

THE FLIGHT OF ENDYMION

So from the turf outsprang two steeds jet-black,
Each with large dark blue wings upon his back.
The youth of Caria plac'd the lovely dame
On one, and felt himself in spleen to tame
The other's fierceness. Through the air they flew,

26

High as the eagles. Like two drops of dew
Exhal'd to Phoebus' lips, away they are gone,
Far from the earth away, unseen, alone,
Among cool clouds and winds, but that the free,
The buoyant life of song can floating be
Above their heads, and follow them untired.

These raven horses, though they foster'd are
Of earth's splenetic fire, dully drop
Their full-vein'd ears, nostrils blood wide, and stop;
Upon the spiritless mist have they outspread
Their ample feathers, are in slumber dead,—
And on those pinions, level in mid-air,
Endymion sleepeth and the lady fair.
Slowly they sail, slowly as icy isle
Upon a calm sea drifting:

... He rous'd the steeds; they beat
Their wings chivalrous into the clear air,
Leaving old Sleep within his vapoury lair.

The good-night blush of eve was waning slow,
And Vesper, risen star, began to throe
In the dusk heavens silvery, when they
Thus sprang direct towards the Galaxy.
Nor did speed hinder converse soft and strange—
Eternal oaths and vows they interchange,
In such wise, in such temper, so aloof
Up in the winds, beneath a starry roof,
So witless of their doom, that verily
'Tis well-nigh past man's search their hearts to see;
Whether they wept, or laugh'd, or griev'd, or toy'd—
Most like with joy gone mad, with sorrow cloy'd.

Full facing their swift flight, from ebon streak,
The moon put forth a little diamond peak,
No bigger than an unobserved star,
Or tiny point of fairy scimitar;
Bright signal that she only stoop'd to tie
Her silver sandals, ere deliciously
She bow'd into the heavens her timid head.
Slowly she rose, as though she would have fled,
While to his lady meek the Carian turn'd,
To mark if her dark eyes had yet discern'd
This beauty in its birth—Despair! despair!
He saw her body fading gaunt and spare
In the cold moonshine. Straight he seiz'd her wrist;
It melted from his grasp: her hand he kiss'd,
And, horror! kiss'd his own—he was alone.
Her steed a little higher soar'd, and then
Dropt hawkwise to the earth.

JOHN KEATS

THE SUPPLIANT'S CHORUS

Oh that I could as smoke arise,
    That rolls its black wreaths through the air;
Mix with the clouds, that o'er the skies
    Show their light forms, and disappear;
Or like the dust be toss'd
    By every sportive wind, till all be lost!'

AESCHYLUS

THE ASPIRATIONS OF CINESIAS

(from *The Birds*)

Fearless, I direct my flight
To the vast Olympian height;

28

Thence at random, I repair,
Wafted in the whirling air;
With an eddy, wild and strong,
Over all the field of song.

.   .   .   .

Let me live and let me sing,
Like a bird upon the wing.

.   .   .   .

Ye gentle feathered tribes,
Of every plume and hue,
That, in the uninhabited air,
Are hurrying here and there;
Oh, that I, like you,
Could leave this earthly level,
For a wild aerial revel:
O'er the waste of ocean,
To wander and to dally,
With the billows' motion;
Or, in an eager sally,
Soaring to the sky,
To range and rove on high
With my plumy sails.
Buffeted and baffled, with the gusty gales,
Buffeted and baffled. . . .

ARISTOPHANES

PHAETON

Meanwhile the restless horses neigh'd aloud,
Breathing out fire, and pawing where they stood.
Tethys, not knowing what had pass'd, gave way,
And all the waste of heaven before them lay.
They spring together out, and swiftly bear
The flying youth through clouds and yielding air;

With wingy speed outstrip the eastern wind,
And leave the breezes of the moon behind.
The youth was light, nor could he fill the seat,
Or poise the chariot with its wonted weight.
But as at sea the unballasted vessel rides,
Cast to and fro, the sport of winds and tides,
So in the bounding chariot, toss'd on high,
The youth is hurried headlong through the sky.

Soon as the steeds perceive it, they forsake
Their stated course, and leave the beaten track.
The youth was in a maze, nor did he know
Which way to turn the reins, or where to go;
Nor would the horses, had he known, obey.
Then the seven stars first felt Apollo's ray,
And wish'd to dip in the forbidden sea.
The folded serpent, next the frozen pole,
Stiff and benumbed before, began to roll,
And raged with inward heat, and threaten'd war,
And shot a redder light from every star;
Nay, and 'tis said, Bootes, too, that fain
Thou would'st have fled, though cumbered with thy wain.

The unhappy youth, then, bending down his head,
Saw earth and ocean far beneath him spread.
His colour changed, he startled at a sight,
And his darken'd by too great a light.
Now could he wish the fiery steeds untried,
His birth obscure, and his request denied;
Now would he Merops for his father own,
And quit his boasted kindred to the Sun.

So fares the pilot, when his ship is toss'd
In troubled seas, and all its steerage lost;

He gives her to the winds, and in despair
Seeks his last refuge in the gods and prayer.
What could he do? His eyes, if backward cast,
Find a long path he had already pass'd;
If forward, still a longer path they find:
Both he compares, and measures in his mind;
And sometimes casts an eye upon the east,
And sometimes looks upon the forbidden west.
The horses' names he knows not in the fright;
Nor would he loose the reins, nor could he hold them right.
Now all the horrors of the heavens he spies,
And monstrous shadows of prodigious size;
That, decked with stars, lie scattered o'er the skies.

There is a place above, where Scopio bent
In tail and arms surrounds a vast extent;
In a wide circuit of the heavens he shines,
And fills the space of two celestial signs.
Soon as the youth beheld him vex'd with heat
Brandish his sting, and in his poison sweat,
Half-dead with sudden fear he dropp'd the reins;
The horses felt them loose about their manes,
And, flying out through all the plains above,
Ran, uncontrolled, where'er their fury drove;
Rushed on the stars, and, through a pathless way
Of unknown regions, hurried on the day.
And now above and now below they flew,
And near the earth the burning chariot drew. . . .

Jove called to witness every power above,
And even the god, whose son the chariot drove,
That what he acts he is compell'd to do
Or universal ruin must ensue.

31

Straight he ascends the high ethereal throne,
From whence he used to dart his thunder down,
From whence his showers and storms he used to pour,
But now could meet with neither storm nor shower.
Then, aiming at the youth, with lifted hand,
Full at his head he hurl'd the forky brand
In dreadful thunderings. Thus the Almighty Sire
Suppressed the raging of the fires with fire.
At once from life and from the chariot driven,
The ambitious boy fell thunderstruck from heaven;
The horses started with a sudden bound,
And flung the reins and chariot to the ground;
The studded harness from their necks they broke,
Here fell a wheel, and there a silver spoke,
Here were the beam and axle torn away,
And scattered o'er the earth the shining fragments lay.

The breathless Phaeton, with flaming hair,
Shot from the chariot like a falling star,
That in a summer's evening from the top
Of heaven drops down, or seems at least to drop,
'Til on the Po his blasted corpse was hurled,
Far from his country in the western world.

ALEXANDER POPE from OVID

MERCURY

Leave the angelic saraband,
    O laughing, lovely messenger,
Feathers on heels, and in thy hand
    The serpent-twinèd harbinger
Of music and ecstatic dreams,
    That thrill the awakened mind and fill
With fantasy the airy streams
    Whereon thou runnest at thy will.

Swift as a star on plumèd shoes,
    Threading the zodiac's wide span,
Pass on, bright radiance, and infuse
    Quicksilver in the veins of man,
And subtlety that laughs at odds
    —Beloved scapegrace of the Gods!

T. W. RAMSEY—Four Witchballs

URIEL

Nigh at hand
Hung high with diamonds flaming and with gold:
Thither came Uriel, gliding through th' even
On a sunbeam, swift, as a shooting star
In autumn thwarts the night.

MILTON

THE MAHABHARATA (KHANA PARVA)

[One of the earliest records of a city being assailed by missiles directed from a flying car occurs in the Mahabharata.]

. . . Mahadeva uttered these words:

Do you now all behold my car, the bow and arrow, as also how I cast down today these antagonists upon the surface of the earth.

The celestials said:

O Lord of the celestials, having taken up all form of the three worlds, we will construct a car for you, that will be endued with immense energy.

Thereupon the foremost of the celestials began to construct that car, which was conceived to be a very gigantic car and also that was, with great intelligence designed by Vishwakarman himself (the celestial artificer).

C

[The long allegorical description of the car is here omitted and the following passage deals only with the flight of the Chariot and the destruction of the cities by missiles from above.]

The day and night were made to be the two auspicious wings on the right and left in that car.

. . . The sky was made to be its yoke; and the clouds its leathern strings. . . .

The cardinal points and the subsidiary directions constituted the reins of those horses yoked to that car.

The traces of the horses yoked to the car were made with the four auspicious days, namely the days of the full moon and new moon with portion of the previous days of the full moon and new moon by themselves. . . .

The cords of that car were constituted by Action, Truth, Devotion and Profit. The mind was the situation upon which the car rested; and speech formed its tracks.

A celestial coat of mail was constructed, that was adorned with the most valuable gems, and that was impenetrable.

O great Monarch, O foremost of persons, when that best of cars was thus prepared by all the celestials with a view to crush down their antagonists (the Danavas).

Shankara then placed his celestial weapons upon the car; and also having made the entire firmament to be his flagstaff, he placed his bull (the symbol of the deity) upon it. . . .

Seeing that car furnished with all its equipments, he coated himself with the armour, and armed with the bow, took up that celestial arrow sprung from the deities. . . .

Thereupon, O Monarch, O King, all the celestials ordered Wind, that foremost of the gods, to carry to that highly powerful Deity his pure and fragrant breeze.

Then having taken hold of the car, Mahadeva mounted upon it, thus terrifying even the very celestials; and therefrom he caused the whole earth to tremble with dread.

The celestials replied to the grandsire saying: . . .

Do you guide the horses of the best species with the object of bringing about the victory of the celestials and the destruction of their antagonists. . . .

Thereupon, O Monarch, the Lord urged those horses, that were possessed of the fleetness of wind or mind, towards that triple city, which was excellently protected by both the Daityas and the Danavas. . . .

When Bhava, riding upon that car, proceeded towards that triple city, his bull (symbol of Bhava) uttered a very excellent and loud roar, filling thereby the different directions with the noise.

Having heard that dreadful and loud roar of his bull, there the descendants of Taraka, who were all the enemies of the celestials, attained to their destruction (died).

All the creatures were filled with terror; and the three worlds began to tremble. . . .

Then having filled his bow with the string, and also having aimed that arrow, and again having united his Pashupata weapon with that shaft, Hara reflected a while on that triple city. . . .

While Rudra was thus standing, grasping his bow, . . . those three cities became united.

Then that illustrious lord of the three worlds, after having stretched that celestial bow, shot that arrow, which was made of the essence of the three worlds, at that triple city.

O highly fortunate one, when that best of arrows was shot at that triple city, there had arisen loud wails of grief as those three cities were trembling down upon the earth. Then having burnt those Asuras, he cast them down in the western ocean.

Thus three cities were burnt and the Danavas were all destroyed by wrathful Maheshwara, who had wrought it having the desire of benefiting the three worlds.

English Prose translation by MANMATHA NATH DUTT

THE AERIAL VOYAGE OF KAI KAOOS

[A translation of the relation of 'The Aerial Voyage of Kai Kaoos, King of Persia', the Cyaxares of the Greeks, from the Persian of Ferodosee, the Shah-Nameh, or King-Book, written in the tenth Century.]

To the King, it became a matter of great concern how he might be enabled to ascend the heavens, without wings; and for that purpose he consulted the astrologers, who presently suggested a way in which his desires might be successfully accomplished.

They contrived to rob an Eagle's nest of its young, which they reared with great care, supplying them with invigorating food.

A Frame of Aloes-wood was then prepared and at each of the four corners was fixed perpendicularly a javelin, surmounted on the point with the flesh of a goat. At each corner again one of the eagles was bound, and in the middle the king was seated with a goblet of wine before him. As soon as the eagles became hungry they endeavoured to get at the goat's flesh upon the javelins, and by flapping their wings, and flying upwards they quickly raised the throne from the ground. Hunger still pressing on them, and still being distant from their prey, they ascended higher and higher in the clouds, conveying the astonished king far beyond his own country. But after a long and fruitless exertion their strength failed them, and unable to keep their way the whole fabric came tumbling down from the sky, and fell upon a dreary solitude in the Kingdom of Chin:—where Kai Kaoos was left a prey to hunger, alone, and in utter despair.

From a Persian manuscript in the British Museum

BLADUD

(Mythical King of Britain, reigned 863)

Bathe was by Bladud to perfection brought,
   By Necromanticke Artes, to flye he sought:
As from a Towre he thought to scale the Sky,
   He brake his necke, because he soared too high.

GEOFFREY OF MONMOUTH
—*Historia Regum Britanniæ*, 1147

II
Prophecies and Premonitions

PROPHECIES AND PREMONITIONS

Perhaps where Lear has raved and Hamlet died
On flying cars new sorcerers may ride.

SAMUEL JOHNSON

KING.   But what a point, my lord, your falcon made,
               And what a pitch she flew above the rest!
               To see how God in all his creatures works!
               Yea, man and birds are fain of climbing high.

SUFFOLK.   No marvel, an it like your majesty,
               My lord protectors' hawks do tower so well;
               They know their master loves to be aloft,
               And bears his thoughts above his falcon's pitch.

GLOUCESTER. My lord, 'tis but an ignoble mind
               That mounts no higher than a bird can soar.

CARDINAL.   I thought as much; he would be above the clouds.

GLOUCESTER. Ay, my Lord Cardinal? how think you by that?
               Were it not good your grace could fly to heaven?

SHAKESPEARE—*Henry VI*, Part II.

A VOYAGE TO THE MOON
A comical Romance

[In 1640, almost three centuries before serious scientists thought to utilize the rocket for a space flight, Cyrano de Bergerac in his 'Voyage to the Moon', sends his hero aloft in a box-like cell, propelled by rockets.]

. . . I went alone to the clift of a little Hill behind our Habitation, and proceeded thus; I had made a Machine, which I imagined capable of bearing me to what Height I pleased in

41

such Manner, that I did not believe there was anything wanting that was necessary to the finishing it; having seated myself properly, I pushed the Machine from the top of the Precipice; but whether my Measures were not properly taken, or that something was wanting in the structure, I know not. However, I fell pretty roughly into the Valley; I soon got up, and retreated into my own Apartment, bruised from Head to Foot; and after having anointed my Bones with Beef Marrow, and fortified my Internals, with a glass of excellent Cordial, I returned to look for my Machine. But alas! it was not to be found, for some soldiers who had been cutting Wood to make St. John's Fire, meeting with it by chance, had carried it off to the Fort; where after having a long time deliberated on its Nature, some of them hit in some Measure on its Use, and proposed fastening to it a Quantity of Squibs, which carrying it by Force in the Air, would serve it instead of Wings, and indisputably give it the appearance of a Flying Dragon. In the meantime, after having hunted a long time for it to no purpose, Chance conducted me to the Place of Consultation, in the very moment that they had set it on Fire. My anxiety at the danger in which I saw my Handy-work is inexpressible; transported with choler I flew upon the Soldier who was enkindling it; and snatching the match out of his Hand, endeavoured by throwing myself into the Machine, to disperse and extinguish the Combustibles which surrounded it; but my arrival was too late. I had scarce set both my feet in it, when the Explosion of the Fire-works carried me and it to the Clouds. To recollect what I thought at that moment is impossible, the Horror of the Accident had transfixed my Soul, and deprived it of every Faculty. I mounted very fast, and I expected at last, when the Force of the Powder was exhausted, to knock my Head against that of a Mountain; but to my great Surprise, my ascent was continued after my Chariot quitted me, which I saw fall to the Earth.

This extraordinary Adventure filled me with unspeakable Joy. I was in Raptures to find myself remov'd beyond Danger and had the Impudence to philosophise upon it. I began now to search, not only with the corporeal but the mental eye, to find out, if possible, what could be the Cause of it, when I perceived my Skin vastly puffed out and greasy with the Marrow which I had used to foment my Bruises. I now recollected that the Moon, at that particular Quarter, having a very strong influence on the Marrow of Beasts,[1] had sucked up that with which I had anointed my Body, which suction acted still more powerfully, the higher I approached her, nor did the interposing Clouds weaken her vigour.

When I had travelled according to the best calculation that I could make, a little more than three-quarters of the Way between the Earth and Moon, I felt myself turned suddenly topsy-turvey, without having perceived the Manner of the Change; of which I was only made sensible, by feeling the whole weight of my Body charged on my Head.

I knew very well that I was not returning to our World; for I found myself traversing between two Moons, the Distance of one of which increased as I approached the other. The larger, I was persuaded, was our Earth, because at the end of a day or two, the distant refractions of the Sun began to confound the Diversity of Bodies and of Climates and our Globe now seemed a large silver Plate. This gave me Hopes that I was going towards the Moon; and my Opinion was confirmed, when I remembered I had not begun to tumble till I had passed three Quarters of the Road. For thus I argued to myself, the mass of the Moon being less than that of the Earth, it follows, that the Sphere of its Activity is of less extent, and the Power of its Centre is not felt at so great a Distance.

At length, after falling a long time, as I suppose, for the Pre-

---

[1] A popular superstition of the time.

cipitancy of the Fall prevented me from being exact, I found myself entangled amongst the Branches of a Tree, three or four of which had broken by my Fall, and bruised my face terribly against an Apple, which I smash'd, some of the Juice getting into my Mouth at the same time.

CYRANO DE BERGERAC

FROM A LETTER SENT BY FRIAR ROGER BACON TO WILLIAM OF PARIS, *c.* 1256

That I may the better demonstrate the inferiority and indignity of Magical power to that of Nature or Art, I shall a while discourse on such admirable operations of Art and Nature, as have not the least Magick in them. . . .

It's possible to make Engines for flying, a man sitting in the midst whereof, by turning onely about an Instrument, which moves artificialle Wings made to beat the Aire, much after the fashion of a Bird's flight.

. . . These all of them (excepting only that instrument of flying, which I never saw or know any who hath seen it, though I am exceedingly acquainted with a very prudent man, who hath invented the whole Artifice) with infinite such like inventions, Engines and devices are feasable, as making Bridges over Rivers without pillars or supports.

FRIAR ROGER BACON

MATHEMATICALL MAGICK

The volant or flying Automata are such mechanicall contrivances as have a self-motion, whereby they are carried aloft in the open air, like the flight of Birds. Such was that wooden Dove made by Archytas, a Citizen of Tarentum and one of Plato's acquaintance. And that wooden Eagle framed by Regiomontanus at Noremberg, which by way of triumph, did fly out

44

of the City to meet Charles the sist. This later Author is also reported to have made an iron fly, which when he invited any of his friends, would fly to each of them round the table, and at length (as being weary) return unto its Master.

Those ancient Motions were thought to be contrived by the force of some included air. As if there had been some lamp or other fire within it, which might produce such a forcible rare-faction, as should give a motion to the whole frame.

JOHN WILKINS, Bishop of Chester, 1648

PRESCIENCE

I, whose Genius and desire hath alwaies prompted me to en-deavour to my utmost, to find out difficult Inventions, do hope at length, I have light upon a way of making such an Engine as shall not only by its being lighter than the Air raise itself in the Air, but together, with itself, Buoy up and carry into the Air Men or any other weight. Nor do I believe I deceive my-self, since I conjure the thing both by certain Experiments and by Demonstration, drawn from the Eleventh Book of Euclid, hitherto thought infallible of all Mathematicians. . . .

Other difficulties I see not which may be objected against this Invention, beside one which to me seems greater than all the rest, and that is, That it may be thought, that God will never suffer this Invention to take effect because of the many consequencies which may disturb the civil Government of Men. For who sees not, that no City can be secure against attack since our Ship may at any time be placed directly over it, and descending down may discharge Souldiers; the same would happen to private Houses, and Ships on the Sea; for our Ship descending out of the Air to the sails of Sea Ships, it may cut their ropes, yea without descending by casting Grapples it may over-set them, till their men burn their Ships by artificial Fire-works and Fire-balls. And this they may do, not only to Ships but to great Buildings, Castles, Cities, with such security that they which caste these things down from a height out of Gun-shot, cannot on the other side be offended by those from below.

FRANCESCA LANA TERZI—*Prodromo ovvero
Saggio di alcune invenzione nuove
promesso all' Arte Maestra*, 1670

FOUR SEVERALL WAYS OF FLYING IN THE AIR

There are four severall ways whereby this flying in the air, hath been or may be attempted. Two of them by the strength of other things, and two of them by our owne strength.

1. By Spirits or Angels.
2. By the help of Fowls.
3. By Wings fastened immediately to the body.
4. By a flying Chariot.

1. For the first, we read of divers that have passed swiftly in the air, by the help of Spirits and Angels, whether good Angels, as Elias was carried into Heaven in a fiery Chariot: as Philip was conveyed to Azotus and Habbacuck from Jewry to Babylon and back again immediately: Or by evill Angels, as our Saviour was carried by the Devill to the top of a high mountain, and to the pinnacle of the Temple. Thus witches are commonly re-lated to passe unto their usual meetings in some remote places; and as they doe fell windes unto Mariners, so likewise are they sometimes hired to carry men speedily through the open air. Acosta affirms that such kind of passages are usuall amongst divers Sorcerers with the Indians at this day.

2. There are others who have conjectured a possibility of being conveyed through the air by the help of Fowls; to which purpose that fiction of the Ganzas is the most pleasant and pro-bable. They are supposed to be great fowl of a strong and last-

ing flight, and easily tamable. Divers of which may be so brought up as to join together in carrying the weight of a man, so as each of them shall partake his proportionable share of the burden; and the person that is carried may by certain reins direct and steer them in their courses. However this may seem a strange proposall, yet it is not certainly more improbable than many other arts, wherein the industry of ingenious men hath instructed these brute creatures.

.   .   .   .

3. 'Tis the more obvious and common opinion that this (flying) may be effected by wings fastened immediately to the body, this coming nearest to the imitation of nature, which should be observed in such attempts as these. This is that way which Fredericus Hermannus in his little discourse *de Arte volandi* doth onely mention and insist upon. And if we may trust credible story, it hathe been frequently attempted not without some successe.

'Tis related of a certaine English Munk called Elmerus, about the Confessor's time, that he did by such wings fly from a Tower above a furlong; and so another from S. Mark's steeple in Venice; and another at Norinberge; and Busbequius speaks of a Turk in Constantinople, who attempted something this way. M. Burton mentioning this quotation, doth beleeve that some new-fangled wit ('tis his cynical phrase) will sometime or other find out this art. Though the truth is most of these Artists did unfortunately miscarry by falling down and break-ing their arms or legs, yet that may be imputed to their want of experience, and too much fear, which must needs possesse men in such dangerous and strange attempts.

.   .   .   .

4. But the fourth and last way seems unto me altogether as probable and much more useful than any of the rest. And that is by a flying Chariot, which may be so contrived as to carry a man within it; and though the streng h of a spring might be

47

serviceable for the motion of this engine, yet it were better to have it assisted by the labour of some intelligent mover as the heavenly orbs are supposed to be turned. And therefore if it were made big enough to carry sundry persons together then each of them in their severall turns might successively labour in the causing of this motion.

⋅ ⋅ ⋅ ⋅

The uses of such a Chariot may be various; besides the discoveries which might thereby be made in the lunary world; It would be serviceable also for the conveyance of a man to any remote place of this earth: as suppose to the Indies or Antipodes. For when once it was elevated for some few miles, so as to be above that orb of magnetick virtue, which is carried about by the earth's diurnall revolution, it might then be very easily and speedily directed to any particular place of this great globe.

⋅ ⋅ ⋅ ⋅

It would be one great advantage in this kind of travelling, that one should be perfectly freed from all inconveniences of ways or weather, not having any extremity of heat or cold, or tempests to molest him, this aethereall air being perpetually in an equal temper and calmnesse. The upper parts of the world are always quiet and serene, no winds and blustring there, they are these lower cloudy regions that are so full of tempests and combustion.

JOHN WILKINS, Bishop of Chester
—*Mathematicall Magick*, 1648

AN ACCOUNT OF THE SIEUR BERNIER'S WAY OF FLYING

This M. Toynard having received advice that the Sieur Bernier, a Smith of Sable in the County of Maine, had invented an Engine for Flying, consisting of four Wings, to be moved by the strength of the Arms and Leggs of the Man that Flys, sends this short Description and Figure of it to the Ingenious Publisher of the Journal des Seavans, who thought it would not be ungrateful to the World, to close the Work of the last year with the Intimation of a Performance so very extraordinary, though the account were very short. . . .

But he [the sieur Bernier] pretends not nevertheless to be able to raise himself from the Earth by this his Machine, nor to sustain himself any long time in the air, by reason of the want of strength and quickness in his Arms and Leggs which is necessary to move these kind of Wings frequently and efficaciously enough; but yet he is confident that from a place pretty high elevated into the Air, he shall be able to pass over a River of considerable breadth, having already done as much from several heights, and at several distances.

He began his Tryals first by springing out himself from a Stool, then from the top of a Table, then from a pretty high Window a second Story, and at last from a Garret, from whence he flew over the houses of the Neighbours; practising thus with it by little and little, till he had brought it to the perfection it now hath.

Now though this Industrious Workman should not be able to bring this Invention to so great a perfection as some may imagine to themselves; yet those that shall be so happy as to bring it to its utmost perfection, will be much obliged to him for having made known these his first Attempts.

ROBERT HOOKE—*Philosophical Collections*, 1679

UNBELIEVERS

Amongst other impediments of any strange invention or attempts, it is none of the meanest discouragements, that they are so generally derided by common opinion, being esteemed only as the dreams of a melancholy in distempered fancy. Eusebius speaking with what necessity everything is confined by the laws of nature, and the decrees of providence, so that nothing can go out of that way, unto which naturally it is designed; as a fish cannot reside on land, nor a man in the water, or aloft in the air, infers that therefore none will venture upon any such vain attempt as passing in the air, unless his brain be a little crazed with the humour of melancholy; whereupon he advises that we should not in any particular endeavour to transgress the bounds of nature, and since we are naturally destitute of wings not to imitate the flight of Birds.

JOHN WILKINS, Bishop of Chester
—*Mathematical Magic*, 1648

RASSELAS, PRINCE OF ABYSSINIA

Among the artists that had been allured into the happy valley, to labour for the accommodation and pleasure of its inhabitants, was a man eminent for his knowledge of the mechanick powers, who had contrived many engines both of use and recreation.

This artist was sometimes visited by Rasselas, who was pleased with every kind of knowledge, imagining that the time would come when all his acquisitions should be of use to him in the open world. He came one day to amuse himself in his usual manner, and found the master busy in building a sailing chariot: he saw that the design was practicable upon a level surface, and with expressions of great esteem solicited its completion. The workman was pleased to find himself so much regarded by the prince, and resolved to gain yet higher honours. 'Sir,' said he, 'you have seen but a small part of what the mechanick sciences can perform. I have been long of opinion, that, instead of the tardy conveyance of ships and chariots, man might use the swifter migration of wings; that the fields of air are open to knowledge, and that only ignorance and idleness need crawl upon the ground.'

This hint rekindled the prince's desire of passing the mountains; having seen what the mechanist had already performed, he was willing to fancy that he could do more; yet resolved to enquire further before he suffered hope to afflict him by disappointment. 'I am afraid', said he to the artist, 'that your imagination prevails over your skill, and that you now tell me rather what you wish than what you know. Every animal has his element assigned him; the birds have the air, and man and beasts the earth.' 'So', replied the mechanist, 'fishes have the water, in which yet beasts can swim by nature, and men by art. He that can swim needs not despair to fly: to swim is to fly in a grosser fluid, and to fly is to swim in a subtler. We are only to proportion our power of resistance to the different density of the matter through which we are to pass. You will be necessarily upborn by the air, if you can renew any impulse upon it, faster than the air can recede from the pressure.'

'But the exercise of swimming', said the prince, 'is very laborious; the strongest limbs are soon wearied; I am afraid the act of flying will be yet more violent, and wings will be of no great use, unless we can fly further than we can swim.'

'The labour of rising from the ground', said the artist, 'will be great, as we see it in the heavier domestick fowls; but, as we mount higher, the earth's attraction, and the body's gravity, will be gradually diminished, till we shall arrive at a region where the man will float in the air without any tendency to fall: no care will then be necessary, but to move forwards, which the gentlest impulse will effect. You, Sir, whose curiosity is so extensive, will easily conceive with what pleasure a philosopher, furnished with wings, and hovering in the sky, would see the earth, and all its inhabitants, rolling beneath him, and presenting to him successively, by its diurnal motion, all the countries within the same parallel. How must it amuse the pendent spectator to see the moving scene of land and ocean, cities and desarts! To survey with equal security the marts of trade, and the fields of battle; mountains infested by barbarians, and fruitful regions gladdened by plenty, and lulled by peace! How easily shall we then trace the Nile through all his passage; pass over to distant regions, and examine the face of nature from one extremity of the earth to the other!'

'All this', said the prince, 'is much to be desired, but I am afraid that no man will be able to breathe in these regions of speculation and tranquility. I have been told, that respiration is difficult upon lofty mountains, yet from these precipices, though so high as to produce great tenuity of the air, it is very easy to fall: therefore I suspect, that from any height, where life can be supported, there may be danger of too quick descent.'

'Nothing', replied the artist, 'will ever be attempted, if all possible objections must be first overcome. If you will favour my project I will try the first flight at my own hazard. I have considered the structure of all volant animals, and find the folding continuity of the bat's wings most easily accommodated to the human form. Upon this model I shall begin my task to morrow, and in a year expect to tower into the air beyond the malice or persuit of man. But I will work only on this condition, that the art shall not be divulged, and that you shall not require me to make wings for any but ourselves.'

'Why', said Rasselas, 'should you envy others so great an advantage? All skill ought to be exerted for universal good; every man has owed much to others, and ought to repay the kindness that he has received.'

'If men were all virtuous', returned the artist, 'I should with great alacrity teach them all to fly. But what would be the security of the good, if the bad could at pleasure invade them from the sky? Against an army sailing through the clouds neither walls, nor mountains, nor seas, could afford any security. A flight of northern savages might hover in the wind, and light at once with irresistible violence upon the capital of a fruitful region that was rolling under them. Even this valley, the retreat of princes, the abode of happiness, might be violated by the sudden descent of some of the naked nations that swarm on the coast of the southern sea.'

The prince promised secrecy, and waited for the performance, not wholly hopeless of success. He visited the work from time to time, observed its progress, and remarked many ingenious contrivances to facilitate motion, and unite levity with strength. The artist was every day more certain that he should leave vultures and eagles behind him, and the contagion of his confidence seized upon the prince.

In a year the wings were finished, and, on a morning appointed, the maker appeared furnished for flight on a little promontory: he waved his pinions a while to gather air, then leaped from his stand, and in an instant dropped into the lake. His wings, which were of no use in the air, sustained him in the water, and the prince drew him to land, half dead with terrour and vexation. The prince was not much afflicted by this disaster, having suffered himself to hope for a happier event, only because he had no other means of escape in view.

SAMUEL JOHNSON—Rasselas, 1759

Alas! can we ring the bells backward? Can we unlearn the arts that pretend to civilize, and then burn the world? There is a march of science; but who shall beat the drums for its retreat?

CHARLES LAMB—In a letter to Mr. Dyer, 1830

The time will come, when thou shalt lift thine eyes
To watch a long-drawn battle in the skies,
While aged peasants, too amazed for words,
Stare at the flying fleets of wond'rous birds.
England, so long the mistress of the sea,
Where winds and waves confess her sovereignty,

Her ancient triumphs yet on high shall bear,
And reign, the sovereign of the conquered air.

Translated from Gray's *Luna Habitabilis*, 1737

I hope these new mechanic meteors will prove only playthings
for the learned and the idle, and not be converted into new
engines of destruction to the human race.

HORACE WALPOLE—In a letter to Sir Horace Mann, 1783

I amused myself with ideas of the change that would be made
in the world by the substitution of balloons for ships. I supposed our seaports to become deserted villages, and Salisbury
Plain, Newmarket Heath, and all downs arising into dockyards
for aerial vessels. In these days, Old Sarum will again be a town
and have houses in it. There will be fights in the air with wind-
guns and bows and arrows; and there will be prodigious increase of land for tillage . . . by breaking up all public roads as
useless.

HORACE WALPOLE—In a letter to Seymour Conway, 1784

PROPHECY

(Written by a Scottish Farm Labourer, 1826)

Wha kens perhaps yet but the warld shall see
Thae glorious days when folk shall learn to flee;
When, by the powers of steam, to onywhere,
Ships will be biggit that can sail i' the air
Wi' a as great ease as on the waters now
They sail, an' carry heavy burdens too.
What else are thae balloons, contriv'd of late,
But th' art o' fleeing in its infant state;
An' if the warld upon improvements fa',
The times may come she'll need nae roads ava;

For wha wad creep like snails upo' the yird,
Gif they might sail the air like ony bird,
Then might folk eithly visit the abodes
O' thae far folk they ca' the antipodes,
Or, by the strength o' steam, yet rise aboon, . . .
An' see what kind o' warld there's i' the moon,
(An' aiblins some o' our earth's ferlies gie 'em,
Or try to carry on some traffic wi' them.)
At least far continents ayont the sea,
Wad then to ithers like door nei'bours be,
Folks then frae Embro, in a morn, might win in,
To tak' their breakfast wi' their friends in Lonnon,
An' the same ship bring Lonnon folks back in her,
To crack wi' Embro folks an tak' their dinner.

ANDREW DUNCAN

THE AIR VOYAGE

A Vision, 1860

Methought I was borne through the measureless fields,
Where the silver moon and the comet wheels.
With a glorious thrilling of joy I went,
And a tide of life through my heart was sent,
As though a new fountain had burst control,
And bade its streams o'er my pulses roll;
 And a shallop frail
 With a shadowy sail,
Hurried me on with a singing gale.

It went through my brain, this deep delight,
With a kindling sense of sound and sight;
And it seemed, as I rose, that the far blue air
Caught a hue of glory more richly rare
Than was ever revealed to earthly eyes—

55

    And still my bark went
    Through the firmament,
As a thing to the walls of the universe sent.

When the car rolled up from the burning sea,
Like a car of flame from immensity,
I felt his beams quiver along my frame,
When first o'er the clouds and stars they came;
And the light dropping orbs I had slumbered among,
Their dim dewy eyes o'er creation hung,
    As each beautiful ray
    Sunk sadly away,
To the inner home of the high-blue day!

Then I sail'd far off to the thundering clouds,
That loomed on the air like spirits in shrouds,
My vessel, sunk on their fleecy pillow,
Seemed a shadowy bark on a dreamy billow;
And I floated through seas of visioned things,
Where the waking breezes point their wings,
    While far below,
    'Mid the lightning's glow,
I heard the dull sounds of the tempest go.

Then storm clouds crossed my glowing track,
And launched me on thro' the hurrying rack,
Till a new creation seemed to rise
In beauty all over the opening skies;
And the spirits that passed on the wings of night,
As they took their farewell feathery flight,
    Poured melody out,
    Like the far-off shout
Of music that dies on its airy route!

G. Mellen

THE CLIPPER OF THE CLOUDS

(Written in 1887)

ROBUR

In the Turner yard at Philadelphia there reposed an enormous aerostat, whose strength had been tried by highly compressed air. It well merited the name of the monster balloon. . . . The dynamo-electric machine, according to the patent purchased by the Weldon Institute, was nearly ready. In less than six weeks the *Go-ahead* would start for its first cruise through space.

But, as we have seen, all the mechanical difficulties had not been overcome. Many evenings had been devoted to discussing, not the form of its screw nor its dimensions, but whether it ought to be put behind, as the Tissandier brothers had done, or before as Captains Krebs and Renard had done. It is unnecessary to add that the partisans of the two systems had almost come to blows. . . . Hence the impossibility of getting the screw into place. The dispute might last for some time, unless the Government interfered. But in the United States the Government meddles with private affairs as little as it possibly can. And it is right.

Things were in this state at this meeting on the 13th of June, which threatened to end in a riot . . . when at thirty-seven minutes past eight there occurred a diversion.

The porter of the Weldon Institute approached the presidential desk. On it he placed a card. . . .

'A communication!' said Uncle Prudent, after taking a huge pinch from the snuff box which never left him . . . 'a stranger, my dear colleagues, asks to be admitted to the meeting.'

'Never!' replied every voice.

'He desires to prove to us, it would appear,' continued Uncle Prudent, 'that to believe in guiding balloons is to believe in the absurdest of Utopias!'

'Let him in! Let him in!'

'What is the name of this singular personage?' asked secretary Phil Evans.

'Robur,' replied Uncle Prudent.

.   .   .

'Citizens of the United States! My name is Robur. I am worthy of the name. I am forty years old, although I look but thirty, and I have a constitution of iron, a healthy vigour that nothing can shake, a muscular strength that few can equal, and a digestion that would be thought first class even in an ostrich!'

And Robur looked the man he was. . . .

'You see before you an engineer whose nerves are in no way inferior to his muscles. I have no fear of anything or anybody. I have a strength of will that has never had to yield. When I have decided on a thing all America, all the world, may strive in vain to keep me from it. When I have an idea I allow no one to share it, and I do not permit any contradiction. . . . And now consider a little before you interrupt me, as I have come to tell you something that you may not be particularly pleased to hear. . . . Yes! I know it well! After a century of experiments that have led to nothing, and trials giving no result, there still exist ill-balanced minds who believe in guiding balloons. They imagine that a motor of some sort, electric or otherwise, might be applied to their pretentious skin bags which are at the mercy of every current in the atmosphere. They persuade themselves that they can be masters of an aerostat as they can be masters of a ship on the surface of the sea. . . . Well now, look here! You are fighting the impossible!' . . .

'But does that mean that man is to give up the conquest of the air, and the transformation of the domestic and political manners of the old world by the use of this admirable means of locomotion? By no means. As he has become master of the seas with the ship, by the oar, the sail, the wheel, and the screw, so shall he become master of atmospherical space by apparatus heavier than the air—for it must be heavier to be stronger than the air!'

And then the company exploded. . . . Was not this hurling a declaration of war into the very camp of the balloonists?

. . . Robur remained impassible, and continued.

'There is no progress for your aerostats, my citizen balloonists; progress is by flying machines. The bird flies, and he is not a balloon, he is a piece of mechanism!

'. . . Besides, with your balloons as good as you can make them you will never obtain any speed worth mentioning. It would take you ten years to go round the world—and 'a flying machine would do it in a week!'

Here arose a new tempest of protests and denials. . . . Then Phil Evans took up the word.

'Mr. Aviator,' he said, 'you who talk so much of the benefits of aviation, have you ever aviated?'

'I have.'

'And made the conquest of the air?'

'Not unlikely.'

'Hooray for Robur the Conqueror!' shouted an ironical voice.

'Well, yes; Robur the Conqueror! I accept the name and I will bear it, for I have a right to it!' . . .

The rage of the balloonists burst forth at last. They rushed at the platform. Robur disappeared. . . .

Two of the most important balloonists—two only—did not seem to think of returning to their domicile. They availed themselves of the opportunity to discuss the question with more than usual acrimony. . . . The dispute of the rivals had reached its maximum. . . . They had reached the centre of a wide clump of trees, . . . beyond the trees was a large clearing.

And if Uncle Prudent and Phil Evans had not been so deep in their dispute, and had used their eyes as they were accustomed to, they would have found the clearing was not in its usual state. Was it a flour mill that had anchored on it during the night? It looked like it, with its wings and sails motionless and mysterious in the gathering gloom.

A whistle was heard. A flash of electric light shot across the clearing. . . . Six men came leaping across from under the trees . . . without a word Uncle Prudent, Phil Evans and Frey-collin felt themselves laid gently down, not on the grass, but on a sort of plank that creaked beneath them. . . .

A door was shut, and the grating of a bolt in a staple told them that they were prisoners.

Then there came a continuous buzzing, a quivering, a frrr, with the rrr unending.

.   .   .

The light had now increased, and Phil Evans could see for some distance within the radius allowed by the frame [of the window].

'What do you see?' asked Uncle Prudent.

'Nothing . . . Nothing but space.'

As he uttered the words the door opened. A man appeared on the threshold.

It was Robur.

'Honourable balloonists!' he said in a serious voice, 'you are now free to come and go as you like.'

'Free!' exclaimed Uncle Prudent.

'Yes—within the limits of the *Albatross!*'

Uncle Prudent and Phil Evans rushed out of their prison.

And what did they see?

Four thousand feet below them the face of a country they sought in vain to recognise.

.   .   .

'Well, gentlemen, do you believe in the possibility of aerial locomotion by machines heavier than air?' . . . 'You ask your-selves doubtless if this apparatus, so marvellously adapted for aerial locomotion, is susceptible of receiving greater speed. It is not worth while to conquer space if we cannot devour it. I wanted the air to be a solid support to me, and it is. I saw that to struggle against the wind I must be stronger than the wind, and I am. I had no need of sails to drive me, nor oars nor wheels to push me, nor rails to give me a faster road. Air is what I wanted, that was all. Air surrounds me as water surrounds the submarine boat, and in it my propellers act like the screws of a steamer. That is how I solved the problem of aviation. That is what a balloon will never do, nor will any machine that is lighter than air.'

JULES VERNE

THE CLIPPER OF THE CLOUDS
(Written in 1887)

ROBUR IS AVENGED

The *Albatross* left X Island in the first week of April. During this aerial passage Robur did not want to be seen from the earth, and he came along almost always above the clouds. When he arrived over North America he descended in a desolate spot in the Far West. There the engineer, keeping a profound incognito, learnt with considerable pleasure that the Weldon Institute was about to begin its experiments, and that the *Go-ahead*, with Uncle Prudent and Phil Evans, was going to start from Philadephia on the 29th of April.

Here was a chance for Robur and his crew to gratify their longing for revenge! A public vengeance, which would at the same time prove the superiority of the aeronef to all aerostats and contrivances of that nature!

And that is why, on this very day, like a vulture from the clouds, the aeronef appeared over Fairmont Park.

Yes! It was the *Albatross*, easily recognized by those who had never before seen her.

The *Go-ahead* was in full flight; but it soon appeared that she could not escape horizontally, and so she sought her safety in a vertical direction, not dropping to the ground, for the aeronef would have cut her off, but rising to a zone where she could not perhaps be reached. This was very daring, and at the same time very logical.

But the *Albatross* began to rise after her. Although she was smaller than the *Go-ahead*, it was a case of the sword-fish and the whale.

This could easily be seen from below, and with what anxiety! In a few moments the aerostat had attained a height of 16,000 feet.

The *Albatross* followed her as she rose. She flew round her flanks and manoeuvred round her in a circle with a constantly diminishing radius. She could have annihilated her at a stroke, and Uncle Prudent and his companions would have been dashed to atoms in a frightful fall.

The people, mute with horror, gazed breathlessly; they were seized with that sort of fear which presses on the chest and grips the legs when we see anyone fall from a height. An aerial combat was beginning in which there were none of the chances of safety, as in a sea-fight. It was the first of its kind, but it would not be the last, for progress is one of the laws of this world. And if the *Go-ahead* was flying the American colours, did not the *Albatross* display the stars and golden sun of Robur the Conqueror?

The *Go-ahead* tried to distance her enemy by rising still higher. She threw away the ballast she had in reserve; she made a new leap of 3,000 feet; she was now but a dot in space. The *Albatross*, which followed her round and round at top speed, was now invisible.

Suddenly a shout of terror rose from the crowd. The *Go-ahead* increased rapidly in size, and the aeronef appeared dropping with her. This time it was a fall. The gas had dilated in the higher zones of the atmosphere and had burst the balloon which, half inflated still, was falling rapidly.

62

But the aeronef, showing her suspensory screws, came down just as fast. She ran alongside the *Go-ahead* when she was not more than 4,000 feet from the ground.

Would Robur destroy her?

No; he was going to save her crew!

And so cleverly did he handle his vessel that the aeronaut jumped on board.

Would Uncle Prudent and Phil Evans refuse to be saved by him? They were quite capable of doing so. But the crew threw themselves on them and dragged them by force from the *Go-ahead* to the *Albatross*.

Then the aeronef glided off and remained stationary, while the balloon, quite empty of gas, fell on the trees of the clearing and hung there like a gigantic rag.

An appalling silence reigned on the ground. It seemed as though life were suspended in each of the crowd; and many eyes had been closed so as not to behold the final catastrophe.

Uncle Prudent and Phil Evans had again become the prisoners of the redoubtable Robur. Now he had recaptured them, would he carry them off into space, where it was impossible to follow him?

It seemed so.

However, instead of mounting into the sky, the *Albatross* continued falling. Was she coming down to ground? It looked like it, and the crowd divided so as to leave a space for her in the centre of the clearing.

The excitement was at its maximum. The *Albatross* stopped six feet from the ground. Then, amid profound silence, the engineer's voice was heard.

'Citizens of the United States,' he said, 'the president and secretary of the Weldon Institute are again in my power. In keeping them I am only within my right. But from the passion kindled in them by the success of the *Albatross* I see that their minds are not prepared for that important revolution which the conquest of the air will one day bring. Uncle Prudent and Phil Evans, you are free!'

The president, the secretary and the aeronaut had only to jump down.

The *Albatross* then mounted to about 40 feet from the ground.

Then Robur continued:

'Citizens of the United States, my experiment is finished; but my advice to those present is to be premature in nothing, not even in progress. It is evolution and not revolution that we should seek. In a word, we must not be before our own time. I have come too soon today to withstand such contradictory and divided interests as yours. Nations are not yet fit for union.'

'I go then, and take my secret with me. But it will not be lost to humanity. It will belong to you the day you are educated enough to profit by it and wise enough not to abuse it. Citizens of the United States! Goodbye!'

And the *Albatross* beating the air with her seventy-four screws, and driven by her propellers, shot off towards the east amid a tempest of cheers.

. . .

And now, who is this Robur? Shall we ever know?

We know today. Robur is the science of the future. Perhaps the science of tomorrow! Certainly the science that will come!

Does the *Albatross* still cruise in the atmosphere in the realm that none can take from her? There is no reason to doubt it. Will Robur, the Conqueror, appear one day as he said? Yes! He will come to declare the secret of his invention, which will greatly change the social and political conditions of the world.

As for the future of aerial locomotion, it belongs to the aeronef and not the aerostat.

It is to the *Albatross* that the conquest of the air will assuredly fall.

JULES VERNE

THE WAR IN THE AIR

(Written in 1908)

. . . [Bert Smallways] was quite involuntarily playing that weird mysterious part—the part of an International Spy. He was seeing secret things. He had, in fact, crossed the designs of no less a power than the German Empire, he had blundered into the hot focus of Welt-Politik, he was drifting helplessly towards the great Imperial secret, the immense aeronautic park that had been established at a headlong pace in Franconia to develop silently, swiftly and on a colossal scale the great discoveries of Hunstedt and Stossel, and so to give Germany before all other nations a fleet of airships, the air power and the Empire of the world.

Later, just before they shot him down altogether, Bert saw that great area of passionate work, warm-lit in the evening light, a great area of upland on which the airships lay like a herd of grazing monsters at their feed. It was a vast busy space methodically cut up into numbered sheds, gasometers, squad encampments, storage areas, interlaced with the omnipresent monorail lines, and altogether free from overhead wires or cables. Everywhere was the white, black and yellow of Imperial Germany, everywhere the black eagles spread their wings. Even without these indications, the large vigorous neatness of everything would have marked it German. Vast multitudes of men went to and fro, many in white and drab fatigue uniforms busy about the balloons, others drilling in sensible drab. Here and there a full uniform glittered.

The airships chiefly engaged his attention, and he knew at once it was three of these he had seen on the previous night, taking advantage of the cloud welkin to manoeuvre unobserved.

They were altogether fish-like. For the great airships with

E   65

which Germany attacked New York in her last gigantic effort for world supremacy—before humanity realized that world supremacy was a dream—were the lineal descendants of the Zeppelin airship that flew over Lake Constance in 1906 and of the Lebaudy navigables that made their memorable excursions over Paris in 1907 and 1908. . . .

But not altogether did she rely on these: she had also a one-man bomb-throwing Drachenflieger of unknown value among her resources.

But the Drachenflieger were away in the second great aeronautic park east of Hamburg, and Bert Smallways saw nothing of them in the bird's eye view he took of the Franconian establishment before they shot him down.

H. G. WELLS—*The War in the Air*, 1908

HOW WAR CAME TO NEW YORK

(Written in 1908)

. . . [Bert] shut the door, waited until the passage was still, then went across to the window and looked out. A drift of cloud made the prospect of the streets and squares hazy, and the rolling of the airship swung the picture up and down. A few people were running to and fro, but for the most part the aspect of the district was desertion. The streets seemed to broaden out, they became clearer, and the little dots that were people larger as the *Vaterland* came down again. Presently she was swaying along above the lower end of Broadway. The dots below, Bert saw, were not running now, but standing and looking up. Then suddenly they were all running again.

Something had dropped from the aeroplane, something that looked small and flimsy. It hit the pavement near a big archway just underneath Bert. A little man was sprinting along the sidewalk within half a dozen yards, and two or three others and one woman were bolting across the roadway.

They were odd little figures, so very small were they about the heads, so very active about the elbows and legs. It was really funny to see their legs going. Foreshortened humanity has no dignity. The little man on the pavement jumped comically—no doubt with terror—as the bomb fell beside him.

Then blinding flames squirted out in all directions from the point of impact, and the little man who had jumped became, for an instant, a flash of fire and vanished—vanished absolutely. The people running out into the road took preposterous clumsy leaps, then flopped down and lay still, with their torn clothes smouldering into flame. Then pieces of the archway began to drop, and the lower masonry of the building to fall in with the rumbling sound of coals being shot into a cellar. A faint screaming reached Bert, and then a crowd of people ran out into the street, one man limping and gesticulating awkwardly. He halted and went back towards the building. A falling mass of brickwork hit him and sent him sprawling to lie still and crumpled where he fell. Dust and black smoke came pouring into the street, and were presently shot with red flame....

In this manner the massacre of New York began. She was the first of the great cities of the Scientific Age to suffer by the enormous powers and grotesque limitations of aerial warfare. She was wrecked as in the previous century endless barbaric cities had been bombarded, because she was at once too strong to be occupied, and too undisciplined and proud to surrender in order to escape destruction. Given the circumstances, the thing had to be done. It was impossible for the Prince to desist and own himself defeated, and it was impossible to subdue the city except by largely destroying it. The catastrophe was the logical outcome of the situation created by the application of science to warfare. It was unavoidable that great cities should be destroyed. In spite of his intense exasperation with his dilemma, the Prince sought to be moderate even in massacre. He tried to give a memorable lesson with the minimum waste of life and the minimum expenditure of explosives. For that night he proposed only the wrecking of Broadway. He directed the air-fleet to move in column over the route of this thoroughfare, dropping bombs, the *Vaterland* leading. And so our Bert Smallways became a participant in one of the most cold-blooded slaughters in the world's history, in which those who were neither excited nor, except for the remotest chance of a bullet, in any danger, poured death and destruction upon homes and crowds below.

He clung to the frame of the porthole as the airship tossed and swayed, and stared down through the light rain that now drove before the wind, into the twilight streets, watching people running out of the houses, watching buildings collapse and fires begin. As the airships sailed along they smashed up the city as a child will shatter its cities of brick and card. Below, they left ruins and blazing conflagrations and heaped and scattered men; men, women and children mixed together as though they had been no more than Moors, or Zulus, or Chinese. Lower New York was soon a furnace of crimson flames, from which there was no escape. Cars, railways, ferries, all had ceased, and never a light led the way of the distracted fugitives in that dusky confusion but the light of burning. He had glimpses of what it must mean to be down there—glimpses. And it came to him suddenly as an incredible discovery that such disaster was not only possible now in this strange, gigantic, foreign New York, but also in London—in Bun Hill! that the little island in the silver sea was at the end of its immunity, that nowhere in the world any more was there a place left where a Smallways might lift his head proudly and vote for war and a spirited foreign policy, and go secure from such horrible things.

H. G. WELLS—*The War in the Air*, 1908

PREMONITIONS

Contemporary opinions on Blériot's flight, July 1909

Are we an awakening people? It is the vital riddle of our time. I look out upon the windy Channel and think of all those millions just over there, who seem to get busier and keener every hour. I could imagine the day of reckoning come like a swarm of birds.

H. G. WELLS—In the *Daily Mail*

Blériot did not get up in any blare of trumpets. In the cold, grey dawn of the morning, before the sun had warmed up things, before it had dissipated the dew-drops, he was in our country. It marks a new era in the world.

LIEUTENANT SHACKLETON—In the *Daily Mail*

A rather sinister significance will, no doubt, be found in the presence of our great fleet at Dover just at the very moment when, for the first time, a flying man passed over that sacred 'silver streak' and flitted far above the mast of the greatest battleship. Of course, such an event suggests all manner of fresh dangers as well as fresh advantages for the future, and it is one more evidence of some absurdity inherent in our civilization that our first thought about aeroplanes and 'dirigibles' should be their possible uses and perils in war. . . . But, for the present, we may content ourselves with thinking of the advantage of sailing through the air at about double the pace of the fastest steamer, and skimming over whole continents, swiftly as the *Flying Dutchman*, and without dust, confusion, or examination of baggage at the frontier. . . . We hope the first thought of our Tariff Reformers this morning will be, 'Where is Protection now?'

Daily News, 26th July 1909

'I DIPT INTO THE FUTURE'

For I dipt into the future, far as human eye could see,
Saw the Vision of the world, and all the wonder that would be;

Saw the heavens fill with commerce, argosies of magic sails,
Pilots of the purple twilight, dropping down with costly bales;

Heard the heavens fill with shouting, and there rain'd a ghastly
    dew
From the Nation's airy navies grappling in the central blue;

Far along the world-wide whisper of the south-wind rushing
    warm,
With the standards of the peoples plunging thro' the thunder-
    storm;

Till the war-drum throbb'd no longer, and the battle-flags
    were furl'd
In the Parliament of man, the Federation of the world.

TENNYSON—*Locksley Hall.*

THE AIR IN 2030

Our descendants will certainly attempt journeys to other members of the Solar system. . . .

By 2030 the first preparations for the first attempt to reach
Mars may perhaps be under consideration. The hardy indi-
viduals who form the personnel of the expedition will be sent
forth in a machine propelled like a rocket; and equipped with
a number of light masts which can be quickly extended, like
fishing rods, from its nose. The purpose of these will be to
break the impact with which, granted all possible skill and
luck, the projectile would strike the surface of the planet.

70

The great problem which such an expedition will face, however, is the possibility of missing Mars altogether; and, having escaped from the Earth's gravitational field, of wandering aimlessly through space unable to find a planet where they can hope for asylum. Such a fate, indeed, may well overtake the first half-dozen expeditions which set out from the Earth to reach Mars. But, one day, a few men may arrive alive on the surface of our nearest neighbour in space. It seems unlikely that they can long hope to survive there, far less that they will be able to return to their home on the Earth. The most for which they can hope, will be to send back across the ether a few messages of information concerning Martian conditions; to transmit the results of a dozen accurate scientific observations before they perish. I should not myself be a volunteer member of that party.

The fruit of their messages, and of their death, will be new expeditions, better equipped, better prepared to withstand the physical difficulties of life on another planet, and bearing with them in their flying machines the materials to erect another smaller machine on the surface of Mars. Into this, bearing with them the records of their experiments and observations, but jettisoning the rest of their equipment and apparatus, the survivors of the later expeditions may retreat, and so hope to regain the Earth.

This outline of the exploration of Mars is admittedly fantastic; but can we be quite sure that it is inconceivable? It is typical of the spirit in which the man of science goes to work when he is faced by a difficult as well as a highly perilous adventure. In such circumstances he values his own life no more than an ant. So long as the human race reaches the goal towards which he strives to impel its reluctant inertia, he cares little what happens to his own life and fortunes. He is as altruistic as the first Christian Martyrs; and, it may be suggested without offence, his altruism is calculated to secure even more substantial benefits for his fellow-men.   At all events we may be sure that, when expeditions to Mars first become dimly practicable, there will be devoted and highly skilled men prepared to risk certain death in the hope that, by so doing, they can add to the total of human knowledge.

THE EARL OF BIRKENHEAD, *World in 2030*

ROCKETS THROUGH SPACE

By all means let us agree that space is far from conquered as yet, and that the consequences of such a conquest are at present the mere play of imaginative minds. But here let us stop. From tiny rocket vessels able to ascend a few paltry miles into the air to space-ships and the acquisition of other worlds may seem an incredibly large step. But in the past, steps equally as large, *for* the past, have been taken. . . . At any rate, let us be quite definite upon one point: that in the rocket there has been found the only known key which will unlock the doors to space; that the key has been inserted, and found to fit; but that at present we cannot summon sufficient strength to turn it.

No one denies, least of all the votaries of the rocket, that a vast gulf will have to be bridged before the planets can be reached.   We may regard this gulf as constituting the un-imaginable immensity of space itself, as a gap in knowledge, or as both.   But the gulf will be bridged. Not only are the plans for this admittedly gigantic task drawn up, but the task itself has been begun. It is true that the plans lack many important details. But time will reveal the full extent of their impracticability, and experience a method of overcoming their limitations.

To those who have taken the first few difficult steps of preliminary exploration, there has come a conviction that the path to the planets is negotiable. So strong has this conviction become that there is no danger that the blazing of the trail will cease. As always when the well-trodden paths are forsaken for the untrodden, formidable and seemingly insuperable obstacles at first appear to bar progress. But as past experience clearly shows, insuperable obstacles have no existence in actual fact. They are mere mirages of the mind which vanish when a resolute step is made towards them.

Yet, in this respect at least, it would seem that the generality of man never learns by experience. Ever since his existence, it must be supposed, man has thought in terms of 'impossibilities'. No sooner is one 'impossibility' converted into actuality than he invents another. It is an unending game of which he never tires.

Suggestions which evoked universal derision a few decades ago are now accomplished facts, and, as if to add insult to injury, facts which are taken wholly for granted. The marvel of the telephone has long ceased to excite wonder; listening to the radio has become as commonplace as going to bed; and aeroplanes drone overhead unnoticed. Yet, just a few years ago, such things were deemed *impossible*.

Practically every invention of note the world has ever seen tells the same story. First, there are loud exclamations as to its fantastic nature and impossibility, followed, as often as not, by a determined effort at suppression. This failing, a more conciliatory attitude is adopted. The impossibility may not be so impossible after all. The next step is to proclaim that the impossibility is not an impossibility at all. And finally, there follow fervent declarations to the effect that there never was a suspicion of impossibility. The inventor is a genius! (Though only too often he never realizes this, having, in the meantime, died in abject poverty.)

And so—amazingly enough—the world has progressed. . . . It may be safely said, cynically, yet with truth, that one of the greatest arguments in favour of interplanetary travel is that so

73

comparatively few people believe that it is possible. Popular opinion, always right in its own generation, almost invariably founders in the next.

P. E. CLEATOR—*Rockets through Space*

III
Balloons

BALLOONS

A spectator, with Benjamin Franklin, at one of the first Montgolfier ascensions, disparagingly asked, in the hearing of the American envoy, 'Of what use is a balloon?' Franklin retorted, 'Of what use is a baby?'

The epigram of the first American aeronautical reporter was prophetic.

GOLDSTROM—*A Narrative History of Aviation*

THE MONTGOLFIER BALLOON

Montgolfier nous apprit à créer un nuage.
Son génie étonnant, aussi hardi que sage,
Sous un immense voile enfermant la vapeur
Par sa capacité détruit la pesanteur.
Notre audace, bientôt, en saura faire usage,
Nous soumettrons de l'air le mobile élément,
Et des champs azurés le périlleux voyage
Ne nous paraîtra plus qu'un simple amusement.

ANON.

THE FIRST BALLOON ASCENT

On Thursday, 5th June 1783, the States of Vivarais being assembled at Annonay (36 miles from Lyons), Messrs. Montgolfier invited them to see their new aerostatic experiment.

Imagine the surprise of the Deputies and spectators on seeing in the public square a ball, 110 feet in circumference, attached at its base to a wooden frame of 16 feet surface. This enormous bag, with frame, weighed 300 lbs. and could contain 22,000 feet of vapour.

Imagine the general astonishment when the inventors announced that, as soon as it should be filled with gas (which they had a simple means of making), it would rise of itself to the clouds. One must here remark that, notwithstanding the general confidence in the knowledge and wisdom of Messrs. Montgolfier, such an experiment appeared so incredible to those who were present, that all doubted of its success.

But Messrs. Montgolfier taking it in hand, proceed to make the vapours, which gradually swell it out till it assumes a beautiful form. Strong arms are now required to retain it; at a given signal it is loosed, rises with rapidity, and in ten minutes attains a height of 6,000 feet; it proceeds 7,668 feet in a horizontal direction, and gently falls to the ground.

> Just as the Omnipotent, who turns
> The system of a world's concerns,
> From mere minutiae can educe
> Events of the most important use;
> But who can tell how vast the plan,
> Which this day's incident began?

From a contemporary letter

GRAND AIR BALLOON

From Paris

Lyceum   Strand

Forty Feet in Circumference

Monsieur Chevalier has the honour of announcing to the Noblemen of England! that the Grand Aerostatic Globe of the immortal Monsieur *Montgolfier* is just arrived in this Capital from Paris, in its Progress to the University of Oxford; and that in order to gratify their Curiosity, this immense, sublime, and most brilliant Spectacle will be exhibited to them for a few Days, before its Removal to Oxford, in the Grand Apartment called the Lyceum, three doors above Exeter Change in the Strand, London.

As Monsieur *Montgolfier!* In the Honour of Science and with all the Liberality of a true Philosopher! has ordained his *Air Balloon* to be shown to the English Nation without any expence, Monsieur *Chevalier* permits the Domestic who has the Honour of superintending it, to receive but *One Shilling* from each Person, to defray in Part the Expences of this Advertising, and of the noble and most commodious Apartment in which it is exhibited. It is hoped therefore that the Learned and the Curious will instantly profit by the public Notice.

This brilliant and most magnificent Spectacle is doubly overlaid with Gold! upon it beam with effulgent Glory, Constellations of Stars, and all the Planets of our Solar System!—and in fine, the whole exhibits the Appearance of a Huge World floating in the incomprehensible Infinity of Eternal Space ! ! !

The Balloon being full Forty Feet in Circumference, if it was in Reality what it appears to be, solid Gold, it would weigh more than Four Millions of Pounds.

N.B.—As the Time is so short, Company will be admitted from Nine in the Morning, till Five at Night.

Vive le Roi! et la Reine! d'Angleterre.

Poster in the British Museum

THE FIRST ADVENTURER IN THE AIR

Scarce 10 months had elapsed since M. Montgolfier made his first aerostatic experiment, when M. Pilâtre de Rozier publicly offered himself to be the first adventurer in the newly invented aerial machine.

His offer was accepted; his courage remained undaunted; and on the 15th October 1783, he actually ascended into the atmosphere, to the astonishment of a gazing multitude.[1]

The intrepid adventurer, returning from the sky, assured

[1] The balloon was attached to the ground by ropes.

his friends and the multitude, which had gazed on him with admiration, with wonder, and with fear, that he had not experienced the least inconvenience, either in going up, in remaining there, or in descending: no giddiness, no incommoding motion, no shock whatever. He received the compliments due to his courage and activity; having shown to the world the accomplishment of what had been for ages desired and attempted in vain.

TIBERIUS CAVALLO—History of Aerostation

THE FIRST AERIAL VOYAGE
21st November 1783

A Letter from the Marquis d'Arlandes, who accompanied M. Pilâtre de Rozier, to M. Faujas de Saint-Fond.

We set off at 54 minutes past one o'clock. The balloon was so placed that M. de Rozier was on the west and I was on the east. The machine, says the public, rose with majesty. I think few of them saw that, at the moment when it passed the hedge, it made a half turn, and we changed our positions, which, thus altered, we retained to the end. I was astonished at the smallness of the noise and motion among the spectators occasioned by our departure. I thought they might be astonished and frightened and might stand in need of encouragement, so I waved my arm, with small success. I then drew out and shook my handkerchief, and immediately perceived a great movement in the yard. It seemed as if the spectators all formed one mass, rushing by an involuntary motion towards the wall, which it seemed to consider as the only obstacle between us.

At this time M. Pilâtre said, 'You are doing nothing, and we are not mounting.' 'Pardon me', I replied. I threw a truss of straw upon the fire, stirring it a little at the same time, and then quickly turned my face back again; but I could no longer see La Muette. Astonished, I looked at the river. M. Pilâtre then said, 'Behold, there is the river, and observe that we descend. Well then, my friend, let us increase the fire'; and we worked away. But instead of crossing the river, as our direction seemed to indicate, which carried us towards the Invalides, we passed along the island of Cygnes, reached to the principal course of the river, and advanced as far up as the Port de la Conférence. I said to my intrepid companion, 'Behold, there is the river, etc.' I stirred the fire, and took with the fork a truss of straw, which, no doubt from being too tight, did not take fire very easily.

I lifted and shook it in the middle of the flame. The next moment I felt as if I were lifted up by my armpits, and said to my dear companion, 'How we mount, etc.' At the same time, I heard a noise from the top of the machine, as if it were going to burst; and I looked, but did not see anything.

However as I was looking up, I felt a shock, which was the only one I experienced. The direction of the motion was from the upper part downwards. I said then, 'What are you doing? Are you dancing?' 'I didn't stir,' said he. 'So much the better,' I replied; 'it is at last a new current, which I hope will carry us away from the river.' True enough, for when I turned in order to see where we were, I found myself between l'École Militaire and Les Invalides, beyond which place we had already gone about 2,500 feet.

M. Pilâtre said at the same time, 'We are over level ground.' 'Yes,' said I, 'and we advance.' 'Work on,' he said, 'work on.' I then heard another noise in the machine which appeared to be the effect of a rope breaking. This fresh admonition made me examine attentively the interior of our habitation. I saw that part of the machine, which was turned toward the South, was full of round holes, many of which were of a considerable size. I then said, 'We must descend,' and at the same time I took the sponge and easily extinguished the fire, which was round some holes that I could reach; but leaning on the lower

F   81

part of the linen, to observe whether it adhered firmly to the surrounding circle, I found that the linen was easily separated from it, on which I repeated that it was necessary to descend. My companion said, 'We are over Paris.' 'Never mind that,' I said, 'but look if there appears any danger for you on your side —are you safe?' He said, 'Yes.' I examined my side, and found that there was no danger to be apprehended. Farther, I wetted with the sponge those cords that were within my reach. They all resisted, except two, which gave way. I then said, 'We may pass over Paris.' In doing this, we approached the tops of the houses very sensibly; we increased the fire, and rose with the greatest ease. I looked below me, and perfectly discovered the Mission Étranger. It seemed as if we were going towards Saint-Sulpice, which I could perceive through the aperture of our machine. On rising, a current of air made us leave this direction, and carried us toward the South. I saw on my left a sort of forest, which I took to be the Luxembourg; we passed over the Boulevard, and I then said, 'Let us now descend.' The fire was nearly extinguished; but the intrepid M. Pilâtre, who never loses his presence of mind, and who went forward, imagining that we were going against the mills that are between Petite Gentilly and the Boulevard, admonished me. I threw a bundle of straw on the fire, and shaking it in order to make it inflame more easily, we rose, and a new current carried us a little toward our left. M. Rozier said again, 'Take care of the mills': but as I was looking through the aperture of the machine, I could observe more accurately that we could not meet with them, and said, 'We are there.' . . . The moment we touched the ground, I raised myself up in the gallery, and perceived the upper part of the machine to press very gently on my head. I pushed it back, and jumped out of the gallery and on turning myself towards the machine, expected to find it distended, but was surprised to find it perfectly emptied and quite flattened.'

THE FIRST AERIAL TRAVELLER IN ENGLAND [1]

From the *Morning Post*, 16th Sept. 1784

LUNARDI'S AERIAL EXCURSION

... A cannon having been fired as a preparatory signal, Mr. Lunardi, having embraced his friends, and all matters being adjusted, a second cannon was fired as the signal of ascension. Insensible must that heart be which did not feel itself anxious and interested at that moment for the fate of him, who intrepidly stepped into his seat, and Phaeton-like, seized the reins which were to guide the chariot of the sun. About five minutes after two o'clock the machine was launched; and as if dreading the course it had to run, and unwilling to proceed, after having mounted about twelve yards, it reclined to its native earth; but roused by ambition and the spirit of philosophical researches, Mr. Lunardi rebuked its fear, and gave its swiftness to its airy flight. He took his seat in the gallery with great composure and confidence on the balloon's being launched; but finding himself too equally poised he readily discharged part of his ballast, which consisted of small bags of white dry sand, and by that means relieved his weight and caused a regular and most beautiful ascension.

His companions in this adventurous voyage were a dog and cat; the latter was destroyed and the dog was almost spent by the severity of climates through which they passed. Mr. L. himself was, of course, affected by the change of elements as may be readily conceived by those who are told that icicles were hanging on his clothes.

[1] Mr. Tytler made a balloon ascent at Comely Gardens, Edinburgh, on 27th August 1784, and was therefore the *first Aeronaut in Great Britain*.

AN EPISTLE TO SIGNOR VINCENZO LUNARDI

'Sent to Mr. Lunardi by a Gentleman well known in the literary world as a compliment to his genius and enterprising spirit.'

Excuse it, bold Youth, if a stranger should dare
To address thus YOUR HIGHNESS as KING OF THE AIR,
For I was a witness, a charmed one, I own,
When you sprung to the skies, and ascended your throne
Amid two hundred thousand good people assembled,
Who felt for your fame, for your safety too trembled;
Whilst you, a true HERO, of nothing afraid,
Took leave of the world, and mankind, undismay'd;
Determin'd to bid every danger defiance
For the noblest of conquests, the conquest of SCIENCE.

When you bid us adieu, and first quitted the earth,
To what varied sentiments gave you quick birth?
Each mind was brim full of unnumber'd strange notions,
Each eye all attention, to watch all your motions.
The multitude scarcely believ'd that a man
With his senses about him could form such a plan,
And thought that as Bedlam was so very nigh
You had better been there, than turned loose in the sky!
But when they perceiv'd you rose higher and higher,
O'er topp'd every building, each church, and each spire,
They extoll'd with one voice your superlative merit,
Who could hazard your life with so dauntless a spirit,
With benevolent wishes each bosom now burns,
And AWE and AMAZEMENT both fill it by turns.

Ah! tell me, Lunardi—hereafter you may!
What new scenes of wonder your flight must display?
How awful the feel, when through new regions gliding,

Through currents untried, and from cloud to cloud sliding?
With what new ideas your mind must o'erflow!
With what new sensations your bosom must glow!
How little, how trifling, must then in your eyes
Have seem'd what BELOW we look up to, and prize!
No more than a mole-hill, the TOWER's old walls,
A Hop-pole the MONUMENT—Bandbox, ST. PAUL'S.

Nay, e'en this GREAT CITY we all hold so dear
As a HONEY-COMB only to you would appear,
All its SHIPPING mere spots, though its bulwark and pride,
The BANK and the TREASURY hardly descried,
The abodes of the Great not discern'd e'en with winking,
And the THAMES but a basin for lap-dogs to drink in.
'Tis the points whence we view things which fix, or create
Our imperfect conceptions of Little, or Great!

But should not to you the great lot be assigned
To establish new doctrines of air or of wind,
Should further Adventurers still further rove,
And pursu'ing your course, your discoveries improve
Yet know, GALLANT YOUTH, that to none but to YOU
Will in England the praise, and the triumph be due,
In the FIRST bold attempt so intrepid who shone,
And show'd by EXAMPLE how much could be done.
Our country will gratefully boast of your name,
And LUNARDI be placed on the bright scroll of fame,
With the warmest acclaims of the Public applauded,
By Philosophers lov'd—By the Muse too recorded!

AN INSCRIPTION

Let Posterity know
And knowing be astonished
that
On the 15th day of September 1784
Vincent Lunardi of Lusca in Tuscany
The first aerial traveller in Britain
Mounting from the Artillery Ground
in London
And
Traversing the Regions of the Air
For Two Hours and Fifteen Minutes
In this Spot
Revisited the Earth.
On this rude monument
For ages be recorded
That Wondrous Enterprise
Successfully Achieved
By the Powers of Chemistry
And the Fortitude of Man
That Improvement in Science
Which
The Great Author of all Knowledge
Patronyzing by His Providence
The Invention of Mankind
Hath Graciously permitted
To Their Benefit
and
His own Eternal Glory.

On the Monument,
Standon Green, Herts.

THE CROSS-CHANNEL FLIGHT

By Messrs. Blanchard and Jeffries, 1785

Those skilful and enterprising philosophers, Messrs. Blanchard and Jeffries, ... determined on Friday morning, January 7th, 1785, to prepare for their voyage; the sky being clear, the weather moderate and the wind at N.N.W. ... Now the awful moment came, every remaining cord was loosened, and this large stupendous body seemed struggling to get loose to float in purer climes. The particular friends of our two Aerial Heroes on each side of the boat, kept it gently gliding on the ground till it came to the utmost edge of the Cliff. Then was realized that famous description of Shakespeare, in his tragedy of King Lear, when Gloster is about to throw himself from the Cliff on the other side of the town:

> '*How fearful*
> *And dizzy 'tis to cast one's eyes so low!*
> *I'll look no more,*
> *Lest my brain turn, and the deficient sight*
> *Turn me down headlong.*'

From a precipice like this let the admiring world be told, that these two men were launched to swim in air—or meet inevitable death; and from this precipice, to the rapturous astonishment of thousands of spectators, these bold adventurers floated safe in the atmosphere, buoyed up by a power lighter than air itself. The sight was truly sublime, the spectators were all eyes, and their hearts all feeling. The serenity and composure visible on the countenances of these two extraordinary characters, the display of two beautiful flags, the Red Ensign of England and the Royal Standard of France, the elegance of the little wherry that sustained the passengers, the expansion of the silken oars, and the stupendous magnificence of the Balloon itself, with the sun-beams full upon them, was a sight which leaves all description at a distance, and requires, indeed, a thousand witnesses to establish the truth of this most wonderful spectacle to the absent public.

The salutations from the Castle, the Beach, the Ports and the Town were general, and gracefully returned by the two Aeronauts moving their hats and waving their flags; this was repeated again and again, whilst, by an almost imperceptible transition, they gradually lessened to the eye. At the distance of about half seas over they descended so rapidly, that the spectators were exceedingly alarmed, apprehensive that some accident had befallen them; but in a few minutes they were relieved from their apprehension by their re-ascending higher than before, though the elevation of the Balloon at no time appeared more than half a mile or three quarters from the surface of the sea. . . .

All future ages must applaud the abilities, and admire the cool, intrepid, determined conduct of these two men, who first crossed the Ocean suspended in the aethereal regions by the power only of inflammable air.

Gentleman's Magazine

THE CROSSING OF THE IRISH CHANNEL BY MR. SADLER, 1812

So on the shoreless air the intrepid Gaul,
Launch'd the vast concave of his buoyant ball.
Journeying on high, the silken castle glides,
Bright as a meteor through the azure tides,
O'er towns, and towers, and temples wins its way,
Or mounts sublime, and gilds the vault of day.
Silent with upturn'd eyes unbreathing crowds,
Pursue the floating wonder to the clouds;
And flush'd with transport, or benumb'd with fear,
Watch as it rises the diminish'd sphere.

—Now less and less—and now a speck is seen;
And now the fleeting rack obtrudes between.
The calm philosopher in ether sails,
Views broader stars and breathes in purer gales,
Sees like a map in many a waving line,
Round Earth's blue plains her lucid waters shine;
Sees at his feet the forky lightnings glow,
And hears innocuous thunders roar below.

E. DARWIN

THE 'MONSTRE' BALLOON

From *The Ingoldsby Legends*

... I shall venture to insert Mr. Simpkinson's lucubrations on a subject to him, as a SAVANT of the first class, scarcely less interesting. The aerial voyage to which it alludes took place about a year and a half previously to the august event already recorded,[1] and the excitement manifested in the learned Antiquary's effusion may give some faint idea of that which prevailed generally among the Sons of Science at that memorable epoch.

Oh! the balloon, the great balloon,
It left Vauxhall one Monday at noon,
And every one said we should hear of it soon,
With news from Aleppo or Scanderoon.
But very soon after folks changed their tune:
'The netting had burst—the silk—the shalloon;
It had met with a trade-wind—a deuced monsoon—
It was blown out to sea—it was blown to the moon—
They ought to have put off their journey till June;
Sure none but a donkey, a goose, or baboon
Would go up in November in any balloon!'

[1] The Coronation of Queen Victoria, 1838.

Then they talk'd about Green—'Oh! where's Mister Green?
And where's Mr. Hollond who hired the machine?
And where is Monck Mason, the man that has been
Up so often before—twelve times or thirteen—
And who writes such nice letters describing the scene?
And where's the cold fowl, and the ham, and poteen?
The press'd beef, with the fat cut off—nothing but lean,
And the portable soup in the patent tureen?
Have they got to Grand Cairo or reached Aberdeen?
Or Jerusalem—Hamburg—or Ballyporeen?
No! they have not been seen! Oh! they haven't been seen!

Stay! here's Mister Gye—Mr. Frederick Gye—
'At Paris', says he, 'I've been up very high,
A couple of hundred of toises, or nigh,
A-cockstride the Tuileries' pantiles, to spy
With Dolland's best telescope stuck at my eye,
And my umbrella under my arm like Paul Pry,
But I could see nothing at all but the sky;
So I thought with myself 'twas of no use to try
Any longer; and, feeling remarkably dry
From sitting all day stuck up there, like a Guy,
I came down again, and—you see—here am I!'

But here's Mr. Hughes!—What says young Mr. Hughes?
'Why, I'm sorry to say we've not got any news
Since the letter they threw down in one of their shoes,
Which gave the mayor's nose such a deuce of a bruise,
As he popp'd up his eye-glass to look at their cruise,
Over Dover; and which the folks flocked to peruse
At Squiers's bazaar, the same evening, in crews—
Politicians, news-mongers, town-council, and blues,
Turks, Heretics, Infidels, Jumpers, and Jews,
Scorning Bachelor's papers, and Warren's reviews:
But the wind was then blowing towards Helvoetsluys,

And my father and I are in terrible stews,
For so large a balloon is a sad thing to lose!'

Here's news come at last;—Here's news come at last!'
A vessel's come in, which has sail'd very fast;
And a gentleman serving before the mast,
Mister Nokes—has declared that 'the party has past
Safe across to the Hague, where their grapnel they cast,
As a fat burgomaster was staring aghast
To see such a monster come borne on the blast,
And it caught in his waistband, and there it stuck fast!'
O fie! Mister Nokes,—for shame, Mr. Nokes!
To be poking your fun at us plain-dealing folks—
Sir, this isn't a time to be cracking your jokes,
And such jesting your malice but scurvily cloaks;
Such a trumpery tale every one of us smokes,
And we know very well your whole story's a hoax!'

'Oh! what shall we do?—Oh! where will it end?
Can nobody go?—Can nobody send
To Calais—or Bergen-op-zoom—or Ostend?
Can't you go there yourself?—Can't you write to a friend,
For news upon which we may safely depend?'

Huzza! huzza! one and eight-pence to pay
For a letter from Hamborough, just come to say
They descended at Weilburg, about break of day;
And they've lent them the palace there during their stay,
And the town is becoming uncommonly gay,
And they're feasting the party, and soaking their clay
With Johannisberg, Rudesheim, Moselle, and Tokay!
And the Landgraves, and Margraves, and Counts beg and pray
That they won't think, as yet, about going away;
Notwithstanding, they don't mean to make much delay,
But pack up the balloon in a waggon, or dray,

And pop themselves into a German 'po-shay',
And get on to Paris by Lisle and Tournay;
Where they boldly declare, any wager they'll lay
If the gas people there do not ask them to pay
Such a sum as must force them at once to say 'Nay',
They'll inflate the balloon in the Champs-Elysées,
And be back again here the beginning of May.

Dear me! what a treat for a juvenile fête!
What thousands will flock their arrival to greet!
There'll be hardly a soul to be seen in the street,
For at Vauxhall the whole population will meet,
And you'll scarcely get standing-room, much less a seat,
For this all preceding attraction must beat:

And there they'll be seen—they'll be all to be seen!
The great-coats, the coffee-pots, mugs and tureen!
With the tight-rope, and fire-works, and dancing between,
If the weather should only prove fair and serene,
And there, on a beautiful transparent screen,
In the middle you'll see a large picture of Green,
Mr. Holland on one side, who hired the machine,
Mr. Mason on t'other, describing the scene;
And Fame, on one leg, in the air, like a queen,
With three wreaths and a trumpet, will over them lean;
While Envy, in serpents and black bombazin,
Looks on from below with an air of chagrin!

Then they'll play up a tune in the Royal Saloon,
And the people will dance by the light of the moon,
And keep up the ball till the next day at noon;
And the peer and the peasant, the lord and the loon,
The haughty grandee, and the low picaroon,
The six-foot life-guardsman, and little gossoon
Will all join in three cheers for the 'Monstre' balloon.

Ingoldsby Legends

ROYAL GARDENS, VAUXHALL
Under the Patronage of Her
Most Gracious Majesty, Prince Albert & the Royal Family.
Open every Evening except Saturday.
Equestrian Aero station!
The Veteran
Green
will make an
ASCENT ON HORSEBACK
with his
Victoria Balloon
on
Wednesday evening, July 31.

Mr. Wardell in thus announcing a Balloon Ascent on Horseback, takes leave to observe that the Veteran Green was the First who ever attempted this Daring Feat having effected a splendid Ascent and safe Descent on the Back of a Horse in the year 1828, being the only Ascent ever made in England under similar circumstances. The means adopted with the animal are such as cannot infringe upon the humane and salutary regulations of the Society for the Prevention of Cruelty to Animals! yet the 'Exhibition' will offer all the much lauded attractions of the Late Ascent in Paris, without subjecting the noble animal to the Corporal Sufferings and Cruel Restraint which have been recently so graphically described in the Parisian Journals.

The subject of Equestrian Aerostation having been the leading topic in all circles, Mr. Wardell deems it a duty that he owes to the Public, and to the intrepid Aeronaut, to offer for perusal the following:

Extracts from one of the leading Journals of the Day.

'Tuesday, Mr. Green made his 99th ascent from the Eagle Tavern, City Road, and on this occasion, the usual mode of proceeding in the car was abandoned for the novel experiment of travelling *Through the Air on Horseback*. The announcement of his intention had excited curiosity to its highest pitch. At a little before seven, he mounted his pony, took his station under the stupendous machine, and set out upon his aerial voyage. The pony was startled by the shouts of the assembled multitude when the balloon first began to ascend, and made several plunges, which shook the rider in his seat; in a short time the animal appeared to be perfectly quiet, and the balloon proceeded in a grand style across the town, and was soon lost in the distance.' July 29, 1828.

'Mr. Green's Equestrian Ascent proved perfectly successful; after remaining up an hour, he descended on Bromley Common, without the slightest injury to himself or the pony, who, the moment he felt liberated, took advantage of his situation, and enjoyed himself most luxuriously among the clover, which he devoured with every appearance of a keen appetite, although he had eaten more than a pint of beans while in the Air.' July 30, 1830.

From a Poster in the British Museum

THE AERONAUT

The popularity of balloons is something curious. It comes by fits and starts, like a stage cascade, or an English sunshine, or an outcry for the legitimate drama, or an exhibition of good pictures, or an overflow of dwarfs, and nigger vocalists, and immense animals. And an aeronaut is a species of perennial grub. In the winter we hear nothing of him, he hibernates with his balloon, in the chrysalis state, without doubt, of dressing-gown and slippers; but no sooner does the fine weather arrive, than he casts his skin, unfolds his wings, and is once more a creature of the air, until he 'shrinks from the breath of the first autumn day'. And then he disappears as mysteriously as the flies, or the pins; which we hold to be the greatest instances of spontaneous evaporation known. ALBERT SMITH

ON THE ASCENT OF A BALLOON

Behold yon silken web so finely spun,
Tho' worms prepar'd the skeins that thro' it run;
With wondrous life inspir'd, aloft it rears
Its form, as buoyant as the starry spheres,
And like a courser fretting at the rein
That serves awhile its spirit to restrain,
See how above those weights, that bid it stay,
It heaves, and rolls, and strives to soar away.
At length the word is giv'n, and with a bound
It surges up, and graceful leaves the ground.
Then upward, upward with majestic flight
It soons ascends beyond the reach of sight,
View'd and admired by twice ten thousand eyes
That eager watch'd its blending with the skies.

J. C. P., 1863

ODE TO MR. GRAHAM
THE AERONAUT

'Up with me!—up with me into the sky!'

WORDSWORTH—*On a Lark*

Dear Graham, whilst the busy crowd,
The vain, the wealthy, and the proud,
   Their meaner flights pursue,
Let us cast off the foolish ties
That bind us to the earth, and rise
   And take a bird's-eye view!—

A few more whiffs of my segar
And then, in Fancy's airy car,
   Have with thee for the skies:—
How oft this fragrant smoke upcurl'd,
Hath borne me from this little world,
   And all that in it lies!—

Away!—away!—the bubble fills—
Farewell to earth and all its hills!—
   We seem to cut the wind!—
So high we mount, so swift we go,
The chimney tops are far below,
   The Eagle's left behind!—

Do, Graham, let me have a quiz,
Lord! what a Lilliput it is,
   That little world of Mogg's!—
Are those the London Docks?—that channel,
The mighty Thames?—a proper kennel
   For that small Isle of Dogs!—

What is that seeming tea-urn there?
That fairy dome, St. Paul's!—I swear
   Wren must have been a Wren!—
And that small stripe?—it cannot be
The City Road!—Good lack! to see
   The little ways of men!

Little, indeed!—my eyeballs ache
To find a turnpike.—I must take
   Their tolls upon my trust!—
And where is mortal labour gone?
Look, Graham, for a little stone
   Mac Adamized to dust!

Look at the horses!—less than flies!—
Oh, what a waste it was of sighs
   To wish to be a Mayor!
What is the honour?—none at all,
One's honour must be very small
   For such a civic chair!—

And there's Guildhall!—'tis far aloof—
Methinks, I fancy thro' the roof

Its little guardian Gogs,
Like penny dolls—a tiny show!—
Well,—I must say they're ruled below
    By very little logs!—

Oh! Graham, how the upper air
Alters the standards of compare;
    One of our silken flags
Would cover London all about—
Nay then—let's even empty out
    Another brace of bags!

Oh! what is glory?—what is fame?
Hark to the little mob's acclaim,
    'Tis nothing but a hum!—
A few near gnats would trump as loud
As all the shouting of a crowd
    That has so far to come!—

Well—they are wise that choose the near,
A few small buzzards in the ear,
    To organs ages hence!—
Ah me, how distance touches all;
It makes the true look rather small,
    But murders poor pretence.

'The world recedes—it disappears!
Heav'n opens on my eyes—my ears
    With buzzing noises ring!'—
A fig for Southey's Laureat lore!—
What's Rogers here?—Who cares for Moore
    That hears the Angels sing!—

A fig for earth, and all its minions!—
We are above the world's opinions,
    Graham! we'll have our own!—

Look what a vantage height we've got—
Now—*do* you think Sir Walter Scott
   Is such a Great Unknown?

Speak up,—or hath he hid his name
To crawl thro' 'subways' unto fame,
   Like Williams of Cornhill?—
Speak up, my lad!—when men run small
We'll show what's little in them all,
   Receive it how they will!—

Think now of Irving!—shall he preach
The princes down,—shall he impeach
   The potent and the rich,
Merely on ethic stilts,—and I
Not moralize at two miles high—
   The true didactic pitch!

Come:—what d'ye think of Jeffrey, sir?
Is Gifford such a Gulliver
   In Lilliput's Review,
That like Colossus he should stride
Certain small brazen inches wide
   For poets to pass through?

Look down! the world is but a spot.
Now say—Is Blackwood's *low* or not,
   For all the Scottish tone?
It shall not weigh us here—not where
The sandy burden's lost in air—
   Our lading—where is't flown?

Campbell—(you cannot see him here)—
Hath scorn'd my *lays*: do his appear
   Such great eggs from the sky?—
And Longman, and his lengthy Co.

Long, only, in a little Row,
　　Have thrust my poems by!

What's Rothschild here, that wealthy man!
Nay, worlds of wealth?—Oh, if you can
　　Spy out,—the *Golden Ball!*
Sure as we rose, all money sank:
What's gold or silver now?—the Bank
　　Is gone—the 'Change and all!

What's all the ground-rent of the globe?—
Oh, Graham, it would worry Job
　　To hear its landlords prate!
But after this survey, I think
I'll ne'er be bullied more, nor shrink
　　From men of large estate!

And less, still less, will I submit
To poor mean acres' worth of wit—
　　I that have heaven's span—
I that like Shakespeare's self may dream
Beyond the very clouds, and seem
　　An Universal Man!

Oh, Graham, mark those gorgeous crowds!
Like Birds of Paradise the clouds
　　Are winging on the wind!
But what is grander than their range?
More lovely than their sun-set change?—
　　The free creative mind!

Well! the Adults' School's in the air!
The greatest men are lesson'd there
　　As well as the Lessee!
Oh could Earth's Ellistons thus small
Behold the greatest stage of all,
　　How humbled they would be!

'Oh would some God the giftie gie 'em,
To see themselves as others see 'em,'
   'Twould much abate their fuss!
If they could think that from the skies
They are as little in our eyes
   As they can think of us!

Of us? are *we* gone out of sight?
Lessen'd! diminish'd! vanish'd quite!
   Lost to the tiny town!
Beyond the Eagle's ken—the grope
Of Dolland's longest telescope!
   Graham! we're going down!

Ah me! I've touch'd a string that opes
The airy valve!—the gas elopes—
   Down goes our bright Balloon!—
Farewell the skies! the clouds! I smell
The lower world! Graham, farewell,
   Man of the silken moon!

The earth is close! the City nears—
Like a burnt paper it appears,
   Studded with tiny sparks!
Methinks I hear the distant rout
Of coaches rumbling all about—
   We're close above the Parks!

I hear the watchmen on their beats,
Hawking the hour about the streets.
   Lord! what a cruel jar
It is upon the earth to light!
Well—there's the finish of our flight!
   I've smoked my last segar!

THOMAS HOOD

COUNT ZAMBECCARI'S ASCENT FROM BOLOGNA, 1804

Before a storm

A bark of beauty on 'the moon's' blue sea,
Winning its way among the billowy clouds,
Unoar'd, unpiloted, moved on; the sky
Was studded thick with stars, which glitt'ring stream'd
An intermittent splendour thro' the heavens.
I turned my glance to earth; the mountain winds
Were sleeping in their caves, and the wild sea,
With its innumerable billows melted down
To one unmoving mass, lay stretch'd beneath
In deep and tranced slumber, giving back
The host above, with all its dazzling sheen,
To Fancy's ken, as tho' the luminous sky
Had rained down stars upon its breast. Suddenly
The scene grew dim: those living lights rush'd out.

ALARIC WATTS

LONDON AS SEEN FROM A BALLOON ON A CLEAR MOONLIGHT NIGHT

August 1901

There were the fairy lamps tracing out the streets, which, though dark centred, wore their silver lining; but in irregular patches a whiter light from electric arc lamps broadened and brightened and shone out like some pyrotechnic display above the black housetops. Through the vast town ran a blank, black channel, the river, winding on into distance, crossed here and there by bridges showing as bright bands, and with bright spots occasionally to mark where lay the river craft. But what was most striking was the silence. Though the noise of London traffic as heard from a balloon has diminished of late years owing to the better paving, yet in day hours the roar of the streets is heard up to a great height as a hard, harsh, grinding din. But at night, after the last bus has ceased to ply, and before the market carts begin lumbering in, the balloonist, as he sails over the town, might imagine that he was traversing a City of the Dead.

It is at such times that a shout through a speaking trumpet has a most startling effect, and more particularly a blast on a horn. In this case after an interval of some seconds a wild note will be flung back from the housetops below, answered and re-answered on all sides as it echoes from roof to roof—a wild, weird uproar that awakes suddenly and then dies out slowly far away.

J. M. BACON —*The Dominion of the Air*

TO A FAVOURITE BARRAGE BALLOON

1940

Gold in the morn I've seen you shine,
    And silver in the moon,
Cherished your beauty, called you mine—
    O more than a Balloon!

For me what varying spells you weave!—
    Now white against the blue,
Now dark against a stormy eve,
    So changeable, yet true.

Serene, ethereal, free you ride;
    They say you are, I know,
To some invisible anchor tied,
    But yet it seems not so;

Rather it is as though borne on high
    By pure inviolate will
You hold your station in the sky
    To bid me comfort still.

Today I walked through (Hush-hush) Square,
    Where oft my footsteps pass,
And dun and dingy you were there,
    Lurching upon the grass.

Penned within privets, planes and rails
    On lawns of sooty green,
With cylinders and huts and pails
    Looking—no, not obscene—

But conjuring up a mixture, say,
    Of whale, deflated frog,
Hot-water-bottle in decay:
    A dismal catalogue.

'Twas ever thus. Stay! I would not
    Be fickle like the rest:
Should auld acquaintance be forgot?
    The heart within my breast

Bids me deny that cynic scorn,
    Bids me ignore my pain,
For on some blissful future morn
    They'll blow you up again.

Once more you'll sail the untrodden ways
    Our London streets above,
And I shall still be there to praise
    And (faute de mieux) to love.

                  J. C. S.—*Punch*

IV
Airships

THE ZEPPELIN AERIAL MACHINE

The interest taken by human beings in their own efforts to fly, or rather to travel through the air, is untiring and incurable by experience. Ever since the first kite was flown, probably on the plains of Chaldaea, the attempt has been constantly renewed, and has always failed; but the steadiness of failure has hardly discouraged, much less extinguished, hope. What the inventors propose to gain by success they rarely or never state, but they go on inventing all the same, and the world reads about their inventions with insatiable appetite and a certain sense of disappointment when, as usually happens, the last Icarus comes to grief. . . . The truth is the imagination is touched by an effort which seems intended to lift man out of the apparently fixed conditions of his being, and men are set dreaming as they would be if they discovered in themselves previously unrevealed powers. If they could fly they would seem to themselves men and something more, the idea at the bottom of the fancy that angels must have wings. That is a rather feeble fancy, Homer and the Hindoo poets having ages ago suggested the nobler one that the speed of gods results from their own volition; but as no-one can paint a thought, the wings have enshrined themselves in art, and so live on. We do not wonder, therefore, that every newspaper in Europe has recorded Count Zeppelin's experiments on the lake of Constance and shall not wonder if he is declared to have 'begun an epoch', to have 'realized a dream', and to have 'affected the future destiny of humanity'. . . . No new force whatever has been developed, and no new application of forces, only such a multiplication of old and known appliances that the car is no longer at the mercy of the balloon, but can make the balloon go its way. . . . Clearly there is no reason as yet for the alarm which has often been excited by the accounts of similar partially successful experiments. There is, to begin with, no grand secret in the matter, nothing which an evil-minded capitalist or ambitious government could use while right-minded capitalists or governments remained ignorant how to manufacture the new weapon. . . . They will be very costly to build, they will take time in building, and they can hardly, when Governments are once awake to their existence, be built in perfect secrecy. . . . The machines cannot carry large bodies of men or large quantities of munitions, and we may, we think, lay aside the idea of their use for a sudden and great invasion as impracticable. They would not be more useful for a raid than heavily armed cruisers are. If the recently passed rules against dropping dynamite from balloons were disregarded they might effect a certain amount of destruction, but not of the kind which Governments seek for because it will help on conquest. . . . As for contests in the air, 'the grappling of the aerial navies in the blue,' that would, even if the dream were realized, make little difference, all governments equally possessing the machines, and the chances with cruisers in the air being the same as the chances with cruisers in the water. . . .

What, then, do we seriously think will be the use of the new machine if it succeeds? It will, we think, have one main result, a great increase of the power of observation both in peace and war. The balloons can be so made as to remain many days in air, and very wild lands, even the regions beyond the Poles, or the sources of the Niger and the Yangtse, may therefore be accurately surveyed. The ice difficulty, the forest difficulty, and the difficulty presented by broken or mountainous country will all alike be gradually overcome. We do not know that the happiness of mankind is greatly increased by such knowledge, any more than it has been by the telegraph, but still it is a sort of duty to explore this little planet of ours, and the Zeppelin machine or an improvement on it will help us to perform the duty. And it will certainly alter one condition of warfare, as it will enable a besieger to see the interior of a besieged city, and all the shifting chances of a great pitched battle over, say, 20 square miles. . . . The Zeppelin machine will be an observatory, heliographing accounts of every movement every 5 minutes. The effect of that will doubtless be to increase greatly the brain-power of any good tactician in command, for he will be able to see the early movements of his enemy, and the exact position of his own widely scattered troops. No doubt the advantage will be given to both sides, but it will be more useful to the one which has the abler and more decided commandant. . . . Science is quite as often malignant as benevolent, but we see no particular reason for regretting Count Zeppelin's new application of old discoveries.

Spectator, 7th July 1900

THE WHITE MONSTER

Last night I saw the monster near; the big
White monster that was like a lazy slug,
That hovered in the air, not far away,
As quiet as the black hawk seen by day.
I saw it turn its body round about,
And look my way; I saw its big, fat snout
Turn straight towards my face, till I was one
In coldness with that statue made of stone,
The one-armed sailor seen upon my right—
With no more power than he to offer fight;
The great white monster slug that, even then,
Killed women, children and defenceless men.
But soon its venom was discharged, and it,
Knowing it had no more the power to spit
Death on the most defenceless English folk,
Let out a large, thick cloud of its own smoke;
And when the smoke had cleared away from there,

I saw no sign of any monster near;
And nothing but the stars to give alarm—
That never did the earth a moment's harm.
Oh, it was strange to see a thing like jelly,
An ugly, boneless thing all back and belly,
Among the peaceful stars—that should have been
A mile deep in the sea, and never seen:
A big, fat, lazy slug that, even then,
Killed women, children, and defenceless men.

W. H. Davies

V
The Growing of the Wings

THE CHARTED SKIES

Before you took the heavens at a bound—
Young airman, with the star-winds in your hair—
You had precursors on the floods of air;
Those deeps no plummet made of man can sound
Yielded a roadstead all the birds had found
Out of creation's morning. Free and fair
Their sails were spread or any mariner
With viking triumph of the sky was crowned.
Spring after Spring they tack into the gale,
The fleets of robins, bluebirds, flying north,—
Who marked the course that these armadas sail,
Who bids their comings and their goings forth?
There where your wings break on resisting tides
The frail craft of the swallow dreaming rides.

C. L. O'DONNELL

Thou, O God, dost sell unto us all good things at the price of Labour.

LEONARDO DA VINCI

LEONARDO DA VINCI (1452–1519)

(The first real pioneer of the Science of Flight)

A bird is an instrument working according to mathematical law, which instrument it is within the capacity of man to reproduce with all its movements, but not with a corresponding degree of strength, though it is deficient only in the power of maintaining equilibrium. We may therefore say that such an instrument constructed by man is lacking in nothing except the life of the bird, and this life must needs be supplied from that of man.

The life which resides in the bird's members will, without doubt better conform to their needs than will that of man which is separated from them, and especially in the almost imperceptible movements which preserve equilibrium. But since we see that the bird is equipped for many obvious varieties of movements, we are able from this experience to deduce that the most rudimentary of these movements will be capable of being comprehended by man's understanding; and that he will to a great extent be able to provide against the destruction of that instrument of which he has himself become the living principle and the propeller.

LEONARDO DA VINCI—*Codex Atlanticus*

You are to remember that your bird (i.e. flying machine) ought not to imitate anything but the bat, because the membranes form an armour or liaison to the armour, that is to say, strength to the wings. And if you imitate the wings of the feathered birds, the wings are more powerful in bone and nerve, through being pervious; that is to say, the feathers are disunited and permeable to the air. But the bat is aided by the membrane which binds the whole and is not pervious.

LEONARDO DA VINCI—*On the Flight of Birds*

It is but a small step from the impervious membrane of a bat's wing to the doped fabric of an aeroplane.

IVOR B. HART—*Mechanical Investigations of Leonardo da Vinci*

LEONARDO'S PRINCIPLE OF THE PARACHUTE

An object offers as much resistance to the air as the air does to the object. You may see that the beating of its wings against the air supports a heavy eagle in the highest and rarest atmosphere, close to the sphere of elemental fire. Again you may see the air in motion over the sea fill the swelling sails and drive heavily-laden ships. From these instances and the reasons given, a man with wings large enough and duly connected might learn to overcome the resistance of the air, and by conquering it, succeed in subjugating it and rising above it.

. . . If a man have a tent roof of calked linen 12 braccia broad (roughly a braccia equals a yard) and 12 braccia high, he will be able to let himself fall from any great height without danger to himself.

LEONARDO DA VINCI—Codex Atlanticus

(Actually the first real parachute descent was made in 1783 at Montpelier by M. Lenormand.)

THE PRINCIPLE OF THE HELICOPTER

I say that if this instrument made with a helix is well made, that is to say, of flaxen linen, of which one has closed the pores with starch, and is turned with great speed, the said helix is able to make a screw in the air, and to climb high. Take the example of a wide and thin ruler and directed violently into the air; you will see that your arm will be guided by the line of the edge of the said board. . . . One is able to make a little model of this of cardboard, whose axis should be of thin sheet-iron, twisted with force; on freeing this, it causes the helix to turn.

LEONARDO DA VINCI—MS. B. fol. 83. v

Here then, beyond doubt, and for the first time in history, we have the principle of the Helicopter.

IVOR B. HART—Mechanical Investigations of
Leonardo da Vinci

OTTO LILIENTHAL

. . . By the gleam of the lantern lit by his work it became first possible to trace a pathway in the darkness, whereon subsequent investigators, equipped with the more powerful searchlights of modern science, were able to open up an unexplored domain.

We are justified in calling Otto Lilienthal the Father of Gliding Experiments. Though his work was not followed up in his own country, Germany, yet it bore ample fruit in other countries, as witness the work of Chanute, Pilcher, Wright Brothers, Ferber and others. Indeed, the modern aeroplane, with all its astounding records of altitude and distance, is the lineal descendant of that ill-fated motor-glider which caused the death of Lilienthal. . . .

A. W. Isenthal—Introduction to *Birdflight as the Basis of Aviation* by Otto Lilienthal

THE EVOLUTION

An important work monopolizes a man and, besides many other sacrifices, claims the whole personality. It fires the imagination of the child, and softly approaches its elected disciple in an alluring, toying way, appropriate to the serenity of child life. But gradually it draws the soul more firmly into its golden nets.

It fascinates the youth, and never relaxes its hold on the adult.

The glory of a great discovery or an invention which is destined to benefit humanity, appears to him the more dazzling the closer he approaches it; he perceives not the thorns in that crown, he heeds not its weight, but his whole life is shaped to attain it.

My late brother Otto and I were amongst those upon whom enthusiasm seized at an early age. A story which was then much read powerfully stimulated our susceptible minds: *The Travels of Count Zambeccay*, an aeronaut, who finally lost his life on the occasion of one of his balloon journeys.

More particularly was our interest awakened by the detailed description and instruction which, in the language of an animal fable, the stork imparts to the willow wren.

The small willow wren happens to meet the stork, and complains of fatigue; the latter, in his generosity, offers him a seat on his back, and during the ensuing conversation, the stork explains the method by which he sails without effort or wing-beats, and how he planes down in a straight line from a great altitude to a distant meadow.

This clear description of sailing flight impressed us with the possibility of attaining such by simple means.

Anklam, our native town, with its surrounding meadows, gave us ample opportunities for observation, since numerous families of storks had taken up their abode on the roofs of the barns, and we often watched the flight of the big, handsome birds. Our interest in the animal world also attracted us towards butterflies, and to complete our collection of these, which was the pride of our mother and ourselves, we did not shirk the weary miles to the 'Karlsburgerheide', nor did we heed the gruesome nights spent in the cemeteries, since there we found the rarest specimens. Still, we devoted the greater part of our immature nature studies to watching our friend the stork on the peaceful meadows of the 'Karlsburgerheide'. Often we would stalk him to within a very short distance and that with the wind, as his powers of scenting are but small, but on suddenly perceiving us he rose, hopping in our direction until sufficiently lifted by the force of his wings.

Even at that time it became obvious to us that rising against the wind must be easier than with the wind, because without some compelling cause the shy bird would not advance towards us.

In 1861, our father died. . . . Our mother fostered in every way our mechanical proclivities, and never refused us the means to purchase the requisite materials for our experiments, however hard it may have been for her at times.

Well do I remember submitting to her our plans for our first flying machine, to the construction of which she readily consented. . . .

Our first wings measured 2 metres by 1 metre, and consisted

of thin beech veneer with straps at the undersides, through which we pushed our arms. It was our intention to run down a hill and to rise against the wind like a stork. In order to escape the jibes of our schoolmates, we experimented at night time on the drill ground outside the town, but there being no wind on these clear star-lit nights, we met with no success.

We were then 13 and 14 years of age respectively, and our flying experiments rather interfered with the proper discharge of our school work. We were both not particularly strong on Latin, and our mother therefore placed me in the 'Realschule', whilst Otto was sent to the Provincial Technical School at Potsdam.

Here Otto was able to satisfy his thirst for technical knowledge, and after a lapse of two years he passed the final examination with the highest honours ever attained by any previous scholar.

We had no associate in our aviation experiments; we felt ourselves quite equal to the task. During the vacation we returned to our old hunting grounds; buzzards, hawks, rooks and storks interested us most, and great was our delight when we saw a swarm of swans outlined against the sky on their migration to their northern breeding grounds.

My brother left Potsdam for Berlin, and for one year worked as mechanic at the machine works of Schwarzkopf. . . . He paid us a month's visit at Anklam.

He brought with him a bundle of palisander sticks, which were intended for flying machine No. 2. I was at that time apprenticed to an architect, and took a holiday in order to assist my brother.

To work the hard palisander wood was no small matter; we pointed and rounded the sticks which served as quills for two wings, 3 metres long each. The feathers of these quills were represented by a series of large goose feathers which were sewn on tape.

For this purpose we had purchased all the feathers which were obtainable in our town, and this is no mean accomplishment in any Pomeranian town.

The sewing on of these quills was very troublesome and fatiguing for the fingers, and many a drop of blood upon the white feathers testified to the damage done to our finger tips.

The wings were fastened to two hoops, one of which was strapped round the chest, and the other round the hips, and by means of an angle lever and stirrup arrangement of the ropes we were enabled to beat the wings up and down by pushing out our legs. The single feathers were arranged to open and close on the up-and-down stroke, and the arrangement worked perfectly. We felt sure that this time failure was impossible. We believed that the lofty garret of our house in Anklam would be the most suitable experimenting room, a belief which was unfortunate, since we undertook to fly in a perfect calm, a method which presents difficulties even to the bird.

We did not heed the lesson taught by our storks, but suspended our apparatus from the beams of the roof and began to move the wings. The very first movement of our legs brought about a jumping at the suspension rope, and as our position was nearly horizontal we were most uncomfortable. When drawing up our legs, that is, when the wings moved upwards, the whole arrangement dropped down and hung on the taut rope. The lifting effect due to the beating down of the wings amounted to 20 cm. This was at least some success, but if our house had not possessed that high loft, we should have experimented in the open, and with a fresh wind would have recorded better results. But the holidays and leave were at an end, and flying machine No. 2 was relegated to the lumber room. . . .

When the war of 1870 commenced, my brother Otto took the field; his comrades often spoke of their chum, who, even during the campaign, never lost sight of the great object of his life, namely, the problem of flight. Full of plans he returned from the war, and I met him the day before the great entry of the troops in Berlin. His first words were, 'Now we shall finish it,' but matters did not develop quite so quickly.

GUSTAV LILIENTHAL—Preface to *Birdflight as the Basis of Aviation* by Otto Lilienthal

BIRDFLIGHT AS THE BASIS OF AVIATION

(1891)

With each advent of spring, when the air is alive with innumerable happy creatures; when the storks on their arrival at their old northern resorts fold up the imposing flying apparatus which has carried them thousands of miles, lay back their heads and announce their arrival by joyously rattling their beaks; when the swallows have made their entry and hurry through our streets and pass our windows in sailing flight; when the lark appears as a dot in the ether and manifests its joy of existence by its song; then a certain desire takes possession of man. He longs to soar upward and to glide, free as a bird, over smiling fields, leafy woods and mirror-like lakes, and so enjoy the varying landscapes as fully as only a bird can do.

Who is there who, at such times at least, does not deplore the inability of man to indulge in voluntary flight and to unfold wings as effectively as birds do, in order to give the highest expression to his desire for migration?

Are we still to be debarred from calling this art our own, and are we only to look up longingly to inferior creatures who describe their beautiful paths in the blue of the sky?

Is this painful consideration to be still further intensified by the conviction that we shall never be able to discover the flying method of birds? Or will it be within the scope of the human mind to fathom those means which will be a substitute for what Nature has denied us?

Though neither the one nor the other of the above propositions has thus far proved to be correct, we perceive with satisfaction that the number of those is increasing who have made it their task to shed more light on this dark pathway of knowledge.

The observation of nature constantly revives the conviction that flight cannot and will not be denied to man for ever.

No one who has had an opportunity of observing large birds, which move through the air with slow wing-beats and often only with extended but motionless wings, especially the large birds on the high seas; of studying their flight at close quarters; of appreciating the beauty and perfection of their movements; of admiring the efficiency and safety of their flying apparatus; and who is able to deduce from the majesty of those movements the moderate efforts and, with the assistance of the wind, the small amount of energy required for such flight, can believe that the time is far distant when our knowledge and understanding of the method of flight will enable us to break the spell which has so far made it impossible to free our foot from mother earth even for one voluntary flight.

It must not remain our desire only to acquire the art of the bird, nay, it is our duty not to rest until we have attained to a perfect scientific conception of the problem of flight, even though as the result of such endeavours we arrive at the conclusion that we shall never be able to transfer our highway to the air. But it may also be that our investigations will teach us to artificially imitate what nature demonstrates to us daily in bird flight.

Therefore let us investigate in a truly scientific spirit, without preconceived notions as to the nature of birdflight, its mechanism, and the conclusions which may be derived from it.

OTTO LILIENTHAL—*Birdflight as the Basis of Aviation*

CONCLUSIONS

... Finally we endeavoured to prove, by actual experiments, that the true secret of birdflight was the curvature of the bird's wing, which accounted for the natural, small effort required for forward flight, and which, together with the peculiar lifting effects of the wind, explained the ability of birds to 'sail'. . . . We perceive how the properties of the curved natural wing push the force factor more in the background, and make flight appear more as a question of skill.

Motive power and force are numerically limited, but not so skill. With 'force' we are, sooner or later, confronted by permanent impossibilities, but the progress of our skill can only be temporarily checked by difficulties.

Let us observe the gull, which floats almost motionless, three arms' length above our head. The sinking sun traces the shadow of the wing edge upon the slightly curved under surface of its wing, usually light grey in colour, but now a ruddy gold; every rotation of the wings alters the width of this shadow, which also gives us an idea of the camber of the wing, when the gull rests on the air.

Such is the material wing, which, in the words of 'Faust', Goethe had in mind:

'Aye, 'twill not be so easy,
To mate the wings of mind with material wings.'

It will, indeed, be no easy matter to construct a useful wing for man, built upon the lines of the natural wing and endowed with all the dynamically economical properties of the latter; and it will be even a more difficult task to master the wind, that erratic force which so often destroys our handiwork, with those material wings which nature has not made part of our body. But we must admit the possibility that continued investigation and experience will bring us ever nearer to that solemn moment, when the first man will rise from earth by means of wings, if only for a few seconds, and marks that historical moment which heralds the inauguration of a new era in our civilization.

OTTO LILIENTHAL—*Birdflight as the Basis of Aviation*

LINES FROM 'FAUST'

(ACT 1, SCENE 2)

(A Translation of the Passage referred to by Otto Lilienthal)

Mark how, beneath the evening sunlight's glow
The green-embosomed houses glitter.
The glow retreats, done is the day of toil;
It yonder hastes, new fields of life exploring;
Ah! that no wing can lift me from the soil,
Upon its track to follow, follow soaring.
Then would I see eternal Evening gild
The silent world beneath me glowing,
On fire each mountain-peak, with peace each valley filled,
The silver brook to golden rivers flowing.
The mountain-chain, with all its gorges deep,
Would then no more impede my godlike motion;
And now before mine eyes expands the ocean
With all its bays, in shining sleep!
Yet, finally, the weary god is sinking;
The new-born impulse fires my mind,—
I hasten on, his beams eternal drinking,
The Day before me and the Night behind,
Above me heaven unfurled, the floor of waves beneath me,—
A glorious dream! though now the glories fade.
Alas! the wings that lift the mind no aid
Of wings to lift the body can bequeath me.
Yet in each soul is born the pleasure

Of yearning onward, upward and away,
When o'er our heads, lost in the vaulted azure,
The lark sends down his flickering lay,—
When over crags and piny headlands
The poising eagle slowly soars,
And over plains and lakes and islands
The crane sails by to other shores.

If there be airy spirits near,
'Twixt Heaven and Earth on potent errands fleeing,
Let them drop down the golden atmosphere,
And bear me forth to new and varied being!
Yea, if a magic mantle once were mine,
To waft me o'er the world at pleasure,
I would not for the costliest stores of treasure—
Nor for a monarch's robe —the gift resign.

GOETHE—Translation by Bayard Taylor

THE WRIGHTS' BIPLANE

This biplane is the shape of human flight.
Its name might better be First Motor Kite.
Its maker's name—Time cannot get that wrong,
For it was writ in heaven doubly Wright.

ROBERT FROST—*A Further Range*

THE WRIGHT BROTHERS

I have often been asked since these pioneer days, 'Tell me, Brewer, who was really the originator of those two?' In reply, I used to first to say, 'I think it was mostly Wilbur,' and later, when I came to know Orville better, I said, "The thing could not have been done without Orville.' Now, when asked, I find I have to say, 'I don't know,' and I feel the more I think of it that it was only the wonderful combination of these two brothers, who devoted their lives together for this common object, that made the discovery of the art of flying possible.

Griffith Brewer—Lecture before
the Royal Aeronautical Society
1901

The person who merely watches the flight of a bird gathers the impression that the bird has nothing to think of but the flapping of its wings. As a matter of fact, this is a very small part of its mental labour. Even to mention all the things the bird must constantly keep in mind in order to fly securely through the air would take a considerable time. If I take a piece of paper and, after placing it parallel with the ground, quickly let it fall, it will not settle steadily down as a staid, sensible piece of paper ought to do, but it insists on contravening every recognised rule of decorum, turning over and darting hither and thither in the most erratic manner, much after the style of an untrained horse. Yet this is the style of steed that men must learn to manage before flying can become an everyday sport. The bird has learnt this art of equilibrium, and learnt it so thoroughly that its skill is not apparent to our sight. We only learn to appreciate it when we can imitate it.

Now, there are only two ways of learning to ride a fractious horse: one is to get on him and learn by actual practice how each motion and trick may be best met; the other is to sit on a fence and watch the beast awhile, and then retire to the house and at leisure figure out the best way of overcoming his jumps and kicks. The latter system is the safer, but the former, on the whole, turns out the larger proportion of good riders. It is very much the same in learning to ride a flying machine; if you are looking for perfect safety you will do well to sit on a fence and watch the birds, but if you really wish to learn you must mount a machine and become acquainted with its tricks by actual trial.

Wilbur Wright—Lecture before Western
Society of Engineers, U.S.A., 1901

1903

... As we were not in a position to undertake a long series of practical experiments to discover a propeller suitable for our machine, it seemed necessary to obtain such a thorough understanding of the theory of its reactions as would enable us to design them from calculation alone. What at first seemed a simple problem became more complex the longer we studied it. With the machine moving forward, the air flying backward, the propellers turning sidewise, and nothing standing still, it seemed impossible to find a starting point from which to trace the various simultaneous reactions. Contemplation of it was confusing. After long arguments we often found ourselves in the ludicrous position of each having been converted to the other's side, with no more agreement than when the discussion began. It was not till several months had passed, and every phase of the problem had been threshed over and over, that the various reactions began to untangle themselves.

Wilbur and Orville Wright—*Century Magazine*

THE FIRST FLIGHT

17th December 1903

At Kill-Devil Sand Hill, near Kitty Hawk, Dare County, N. Carolina

On Dec. 17th, 1903, the machine was taken out; in addition to Wilbur and Orville Wright, there were present five spectators. ... A general invitation had been given to practically all the residents in the vicinity, but the Kill Devil district is a cold area in December, and history had recorded so many experiments in which machines had failed to leave the ground that between temperature and scepticism only these five risked a waste of their time.

126

And these five were in at the greatest conquest man has made since James Watt evolved the steam-engine—perhaps even a greater conquest than that of Watt. . . . The faith that had inspired the long roll of pioneers, from da Vinci onwards, was justified at last.

E. C. VIVIAN—*History of Aeronautics*

THE FIRST AEROPLANE FLIGHT

During the night of December 16th, 1903, a strong cold wind blew from the north. When we arose on the morning of the 17th, the puddles of water, which had been standing about camp since the recent rains, were covered with ice. The wind had a velocity of 22 to 27 miles an hour. We thought it would die down before long, but when 10 o'clock arrived, and the wind was as brisk as ever, we decided that we had better get the machine out. . . .

Wilbur, having used his turn in the unsuccessful attempt on the 14th, the right and the first trial belonged to me. Wilbur ran at the side, holding the wings to balance it on the track. The machine, facing a 27-mile wind, started very slowly. Wilbur was able to stay with it until it lifted from the track after a 40-foot run.

The course of the flight up and down was exceedingly erratic. The control of the front rudder was difficult. As a result, the machine would rise suddenly to about ten feet, and then as suddenly dart for the ground. A sudden dart when a little over 120 feet from the point at which it rose into the air, ended the flight.

This flight lasted only 12 seconds, but it was nevertheless the first in the history of the world in which a machine carrying a man had raised itself by its own power into the air in full flight, had sailed forward without reduction of speed, and had finally landed at a point as high as that from which it started.

ORVILLE WRIGHT—U.S.A. Air Service Report

PRELUDE TO ICAROS

The Wrights' first successful flight

There was wind, there were clouds; but they set out the wooden track
On the level in front of the camp; and the weights and the pulleys.
Then the *Flyer* was brought from its shed and shook in the gusts;
It leaped like a living thing as they took it down-wind,
And set it firm on the rail and started the motor;
Long warning, this time: dull roar and the streamers of smoke;
The exhaust-pipes barking; the shakes of the separate parts—
Cams, pistons and gears; the flanges of cylinder shells;
The crankshaft set on its bearings; the chains and the oil—
All growing mellow with heat, uniting and blending;
Adjustments of differing metals—harmonious whole.
Then Orville squeezed through the wires and stretched out on the wing;
He tested the cradle-controls and tripped the release.
Slowly the kite moved off in the grip of the wind.
It crept like a snail; it lurched like a clumsy duck;
It was drunk on the wind—and Wilbur could easily walk there
And steady the wing with his hand; but soon he was running—
His legs were soon pumping like pistons, his coat-tails flying.
Then the *Flyer* pulled out of his hand. The mouths of the watchers
Were dry with excitement and wind. The *Flyer* teetered;
It bumped on the wooden rail; it slewed and came straight.
Then it rose from the rail. None spoke at all as it lifted.
They stood there, glued to the sand, their hearts in their eyes.
It lifted. The skids were clear. It was clear of the sand.

JOHN WILLIAMS ANDREWS—*Prelude to Icaros*

1905

It is evident that the limits of speed have not as yet been closely approached in the flyers already built, and that in matter of distance, the possibilities are even more encouraging. Even in the existing state of the art it is easy to design a practical and durable flyer that will carry an operator and supplies of fuel for a flight of over 500 miles at a speed of 50 miles an hour.

WILBUR and ORVILLE WRIGHT—*Navigating the Air*

FLIGHTS IN 1905 OF THE WRIGHT BROTHERS

DAYTON, OHIO,
Nov. 25, 1906.

Aero Club of America,
New York City.

DEAR SIR,

The brothers, Wilbur and Orville Wright, have lived from childhood within a few squares of my home and have always had the fullest confidence of all their neighbours and acquaintances; but I must confess that when I read that they had solved the problem of human flight down on the coast of North Carolina I did not believe it. I thought that what they had accomplished was not real flight at all, but due to some peculiar condition of the atmosphere in that locality. I believed mechanical flight as impossible as perpetual motion.

It was not until I saw one of their flights, near Dayton, with my own eyes that every doubt was removed.

I was on the ground and stood within a few feet of the machine while preparations were being made for the flight. I saw the machine start on the track upon which it acquired initial speed, and I watched it as it gradually rose higher and higher in the air.

I

I simply cannot describe my feelings during the first few minutes. When it was well above the tree-tops it continued on a level course in easy circles about the field, for more than half an hour, as timed by several spectators present.

The operator brought it to the ground without any damage whatever, directly in front of the building in which it was housed. I had seen the eighth wonder of the world.

Respectfully yours,

HENRY WEBBERS

DAYTON, OHIO,
Nov. 24, 1906

Aero Club of America,
    New York.

DEAR SIR,

I take great pleasure in answering your letter of Nov. 21, 1906.

Along with some friends, I had the privilege of witnessing a flight of the Wright Brothers, in the autumn of 1905, a few miles east of Dayton. The machine started from a short track lying on the ground, and rose into the air on an inclined path till it was well above the height of the tallest trees. It then kept on a horizontal path flying round and round the meadow in circles about a quarter of a mile in diameter.

The flight lasted more than half an hour. At last Mr. Orville Wright shut off the power and landed as gracefully as a bird just in front of the building in which the machine was kept. I can only say that it was the most wonderful sight of all my life. I was astonished to see farmers, driving home from the city, stop and watch the flight for 10 or 15 minutes, and then drive on again; but I suppose they lived near-by and had seen the machine in flight many times before.

Yours respectfully,

CHAS. WEBBERT

Aero Club of America—*Navigating the Air*

AN ACCOUNT OF THE FIRST CROSS-CHANNEL FLIGHT

26th July 1909

At 4.30 we could see all round. Daylight had come. M. le Blanc endeavoured to see the coast of England, but could not. A light breeze from the S.W. was blowing. The air was clear. Everything was prepared. I was dressed as I am at this moment, a 'khaki' jacket lined with wool for warmth over my tweed clothes and beneath my engineer's suit of blue overalls. My close-fitting cap was fastened over my head and ears. I had neither eaten nor drunk anything since I rose. My thoughts were only upon the flight and my determination to accomplish it this morning. 4.35! *Tout est prêt!* Le Blanc gives the signal and in an instant I am in the air, my engine making 1,200 revolutions—almost its highest speed—in order that I may get quickly over the telegraph wires along the edge of the cliff. As soon as I am over the cliff, I reduce my speed. There is now no need to force my engine.

I begin my flight, steady and sure, towards the Coast of England. I have no apprehensions, no sensations, *pas du tout*. The *Escopette* has seen me. She is driving ahead at full speed. She makes perhaps 42 kilometres (about 26 miles) an hour. What matters? I am making at least 68 kilometres (42½ miles). Rapidly I overtake her, travelling at a height of 80 metres (about 250 feet). The moment is supreme, yet I surprise myself by feeling no exultation. Below me is the sea, the surface disturbed by the wind, which is now freshening. The motion of the waves beneath me is not pleasant. I drive on. 10 minutes have gone. I have passed the destroyer, and I turn my head to see whether I am proceeding in the right direction. I am amazed. There is nothing to be seen, neither the torpedo-destroyer, nor France, nor England. I am alone, I can see nothing at all—*rien du tout!* For 10 minutes I am lost. It is a strange position to be alone, unguided, without compass, in the air over the middle of the Channel. I touch nothing. My hands and feet rest lightly on the levers. I let the aeroplane take its own course. I care not whither it goes. For 10 minutes I continue, neither rising nor falling, nor turning. And then, 20 minutes after I have left the French coast, I see the green cliffs of Dover, the Castle, and away to the west the spot where I had intended to land. What can I do? It is evident that the wind has taken me out of my course. I am almost at St. Margaret's Bay, and going in the direction of the Goodwin Sands.

Now it is time to attend to the steering. I press the lever with my foot and turn easily toward the west, reversing the direction in which I am travelling. Now indeed, I am in difficulties, for the wind here by the cliffs is much stronger, and my speed is reduced as I fight against it. Yet my beautiful aeroplane responds. Still steadily I fly westwards, hoping to cross the harbour and reach the Shakespeare cliff. Again the wind blows. I see an opening in the cliff. Although I am confident that I can continue for an hour and a half, that I might indeed return to Calais, I cannot resist the opportunity to make a landing upon this green spot. Once more I turn my aeroplane, and, describing a half-circle, I enter the opening and find myself again over dry land. Avoiding the red buildings on my right, I attempt a landing; but the wind catches me and whirls me round two or three times. At once I stop my motor, and instantly the machine falls straight upon the land from a height of 20 metres (65 feet). In two or three seconds I am safe upon your shore. Soldiers in khaki run up, and a policeman. Two of my compatriots are on the spot. They kiss my cheeks. The conclusion of my flight overwhelms me.

LOUIS BLÉRIOT—*Daily Mail*, 26th July 1909

CROSS-CHANNEL FLIGHTS

It is vital to the safety of the nation, that Britain should become a nation of aviators. In matters of defence, we live on an island no longer. The day that Blériot flew the Channel marked the end of the our insular safety, and the beginning of the time when Britain must seek another form of defence beside its ships.

Sir Alan Cobham—*Skyways*

FLYING MACHINES

By The Little Stint

When Blériot the Channel flew
The people made a great to-do;
They came in thousands just to stare
At the great Conqueror of the Air
Who crossed from France to England's shore,
A flight of twenty miles or more.
'How great an aeroplane!' they said,
'And what a noise the engine made!'
'And how could Blériot know that he
Would find his way across the sea,
Which none had ever flown before?'
And so they wonder more and more,
Until at last their hats they raise
And cheer to their great hero's praise.
Yet I, when called to make my flight,
Have slipped off in an Arctic night
And lightly flown o'er land and sea,
The only engine carrying me
My heart, no bigger than a shilling,
Which for twelve thousand miles is willing.
Less than two ounces is my weight,
No petrol cans increase my freight;

133

No chart nor compass 'neath my eyes
To mark the track through trackless skies—
And still untiring to the verge
Of Australasian ocean's surge
From North Siberia's coast I fly,
Spanning the globe unerringly.
No cheering thousands when I land,
No startling posters in the Strand;
No wondering word, no praise is heard,
But then—I only am a bird.

Punch

AT THE RHEIMS AVIATION MEETING, 1909

... On the grass, beyond the sheds, stood the Farman biplane —the second or third ever built; such a craft as only in museums can be seen today, but for those days, the days of the box-kite Voisins, a thing of grace and beauty. The two planes, 35 feet long, were mounted on a chassis between the four wheels of which, strapped to their axles by broad elastic bands, were long, curious, wooden sledge-runners or skids—one of Farman's special features. Four long, converging outrigger spars formed the 'fuselage', carrying, 14 feet behind, the square 'empennage', in which were two vertical rudders. Four other outriggers carried, far out in front, the elevator plane, 15 feet long. 'Aileron' flaps hung down from the rear edges of both planes (like washing on a line, somebody said). On the lower plane was mounted the engine, its screw-propeller behind; and in front of it, right on the edge of the plane, was the little basket seat of the pilot.

The lower plane was 5 feet from the ground, and there was no step to help one up. How I got up I do not know, and what I sat on I do not comprehend. I was only conscious that Sommer, when he scrambled in after me, was very close in front, wedging me tightly between himself and the extremely hot radiator of the engine behind. I was his first passenger, of either sex, and passenger flight had not been contemplated or arranged for. One word of warning he conveyed to me—not to touch his arms. Then the mechanic swung the propeller, the engine, already hot with recent flight, started with the first turn, and we were off across the track.

The ground was very rough and hard, and as we tore along, at an increasing pace that was very soon greater than any motor I had yet been in, I expected to be jerked and jolted. But the motion was wonderfully smooth—smoother yet—and then—! Suddenly there had come into it a new, indescribable quality— a lift—a lightness—a life! Very many there are now who know that feeling: that glorious, gliding sense that the sea-bird has known this million years, and which man so long and so vainly envied it, and which, even now, familiarity can never rob of its charm. But picture, if you can, what it meant for the first time; when all the world of Aviation was young and fresh and untried; when to rise at all was a glorious adventure, and to find oneself flying swiftly in the air, the too-good-to-be-true realization of a life-long dream. You wonderful aerial record breakers of today and of the years to come, whose exploits I may only marvel at and envy, I have experienced something that can never be yours and can never be taken away from me—the rapture, the glory and the glamour of 'the very beginning'.

GERTRUDE BACON—*Memories of Land and Sky*

THE FIRST DOUBLE CROSSING OF THE CHANNEL BY THE HON. C. S. ROLLS

1st June 1910

For two weeks I had been waiting at Calais to guide Rolls to a landing place and to check the flight. . . . Besides signalling Rolls I had to send a report to the *Times*. This I did, and was astonished to see the following in the *Star* the next day!

'The Calais correspondent of the *Times* sends a description of what he saw of the flying Rolls. Without any alteration of the diction, it might be set forth in Whitmanese lines, paraphrasing the words of the prophet of Iddo's line in King Darius's day, "Then I turned, and lifted up mine eyes, and looked, and behold, flying Rolls!"

Thus:

With our binoculars glued to our eyes,

We watched the airman's progress.

It was a fascinating task.

There was the great expanse of sea and sky. To the right a
    cluster of warships marked the scene

Of the sunken submarine[1]

And the operations for its salvage, a saddening and gloomy
    reminder of the perils of the sea.

A dazzling sun cut a path of burnished brass to the horizon.

The heavens were alight with the tenderest hues of green,

Blue,

Orange,

Mauve.

There was a curious rainbow effect of cirrus clouds.

High in the west, and, right against it,

There was the aeroplane speeding to its goal,

Alone in the great expanse.

Our hearts trembled at the thought of the vagaries of a motor.

There was still no sign of the torpedo-boats that were to attend
    the flight.

Mr. Rolls's course

Was clearly too westerly.

For half an hour he could be seen by the naked eye, but with
    binoculars, until 7.53.

We clearly saw him for 45 minutes of his return journey.

---

[1] A French submarine had sunk two or three days before off Calais with the loss of all hands.

At length the aeroplane became the merest speck 20 miles
   away.
We believed we saw him descending.
Towards the end his course took him nearer
The crimsoning glory of the sun, and he vanished finally
Under a haze.'

   Needless to say, when I spelt out my message on the French
telegram form, nothing was further from my thoughts than
Whitman's or any other poet's style.

C. C. TURNER—*Old Flying Days*

THE FIRST AIRMAN

'Illi robur et aes triplex
Circa pectus erat.'

HORACE

When man learned first to fly
At venture in the sky,
Borne above earth's rude crust
Rather by faith and trust
Than by mechanic skill,
How strange the sudden thrill
That then his soul possessed.
On earth he knew not rest,
But in the fine air found
Joys that the humble ground
Held not: he was the first
To quench the spirit's thirst
For flight, the first to be
Borne upon wings, or free
From crabbèd earth to soar,
To steer for the fair floor
Of Heaven: the first to feel
Such peril, and to steel

His heart to hazard there,
Alone in the strange air.
He held his life as nought,
In the grim fight he fought
To build a way to heaven,
And by the planets seven
To carve a course, to pave
A path above the wave,
A road under the stars.
So he fell, and his scars
Gave glory to his line,
That it seemed half divine
Henceforth to fly and face
The awe of unknown space,
The unmapped maze of night,
Strange seas of blinding light,
Strange sounds, strange sights, and strange
Ways beyond death or change.

E. Vine Hall—*In Full Flight*

REASONS FOR FLYING

If the art of Flying were brought to Perfection; the use that I should make of it, would be to attend the sun round the World, and pursue the Spring through every Sign of the Zodiac.

The Editor of the *Guardian*, August 1713

I want to learn to fly because I want to be able to feel at home in the air—that new element that the pioneers of my generation have made possible for man. I feel I want to have my share, however small, in this new inheritance.

Filson Young—*Growing Wings*

AN EARLY FLYING LESSON

11th April 1911

There were no dual-control machines and really very little was known about flying.

The pupil of today does not experience, but doubtless he can imagine, what it feels like to be put in charge of an aeroplane for the first time, and when you have never had your feet on the rudder control, and only know it by theory; when your only practical acquaintance with flying is that of sitting behind a pilot and holding your hand over his. You know where the switch is, and the petrol tap, and throttle. There were no instruments, not even an air-speed indicator, not even a revs. counter (we used to make a rough computation of the revs. by counting the throbs of the head of oil in the oil-gauge!)

The mechanic starts up the propeller and you hear your own voice say 'Contact', 'Switch off', 'Contact', 'Off', until the propeller runs and the mechanic steps back. You know the moment has arrived, and you have got to raise that right hand of yours as a signal to the mechanics who are hanging on to the machine to let go. And then there is nothing for it: you've either got to attempt that flight, or else to switch off, turn off the petrol, step out of the machine and say that on the whole you think you had better give up this silly idea of flying. Well, of course you cannot do that.

Up went my right hand, and the machine began to move forward. I managed to keep it straight, and the business had been so well drilled into me that at the right moment, when I could see the ground sweeping at the usual rate, I kicked off with the very slightest preliminary depression of the elevator followed by an instant pulling back of the lever. The machine was off the ground; but good heavens! I was not going straight! Wobbling from left to right and right to left! After all, my hands were the hands of a clodhopper; and there was the end of the ground: I had got to come down somehow from my lofty thirty feet or so! I switched off in panic, and came to a stop on the ground, looking about me in bewilderment as I realised that I had not wrecked the machine. There I waited for the arrival of the doubtless agitated and mocking school and an indignant Jullerot. Instead:

'Very good, old chap. Now we'll turn you round, and you must do it again.' Phew!

I kept straighter at the second try except for a tendency to charge into the sheds: and still my sensations were wildly confused, and I did not believe I was learning anything, in spite of M. Jullerot's assurances.

And what a night I had thinking it over!

C. C. TURNER—*Old Flying Days*

HEDGE-HOPPING

10.15–11, 2nd August

There was a north wind and the sky was grey with an overcast sky. Directly I was up, I ran into the mist and began to feel myself lost. After the first landing, I went round two or three times, keeping low all the time and landing well. Then Marshall suggested low flying since conditions were so disagreeable, and we set off. As I got abreast of Girton, Marshall told me to go lower as we were getting lost in clouds, although we were below 300 feet. So I came down low, picked up the Huntingdon road and flew along it. I held the stick forward, nosing down and towards the road to counteract the drift of the wind. It was marvellous. I was aware, because of the nearness of the earth, of the roaring machine, headlong, hurtling racing over the surface of the earth. Sometimes I brought her really very low, and then as I saw trees looming up ahead, lifted her.

At Hilton, I did two turns round the house. I had no eyes for possible members of my family, but only for the elms as I roared off about twice their height.

With the wind behind us on the way back, we were going at the hell of a lick—about 120 miles an hour over the ground, so it was not long before hideous Girton heaved in view. I took her up a bit as I cut across to Chesterton. I shut off and brought her round perfectly to a good landing. 'Time for one more circuit.'

We took off all right, but over the elms the engine missed. Marshall throttled back, took over and lifted her up so steeply that I spoke my thought: 'What *are* you up to?'

He was gaining height for a conk out. Then he did a right hand turn, shut the throttle and sang out: 'You've got her.'

I took her in and landed. I was drunk with air. I was wild and driving home sang and shouted, full of realization that we have found a new freedom—a new Ocean. For thousands of years we have crawled or run on the earth, or paddled across the seas, and all the while there has been this great ocean just over our heads in which at last we sail with joy. The longing for the sea: the call of the sea, one has heard of that, and that was the natural adventure in the past. But now it is a longing for the air, to go up. The air is more marvellous than any sea, it holds more beauty, more joy than any Pacific swell or South Sea lagoon.

DAVID GARNETT—*A Rabbit in the Air*

THE CALL OF THE AIR

Have you ever sat in crystal space, enjoying the sensations
   of an eagle hovered high above the earth,
gazing down on man's ridiculous and infantile creations
   and judging them according to their worth?
Have you looked upon a basin small enough to wash your face in,
   with a few toy-ships collected by the shore,

and then realised with wonder that if those toys go under
  nine tenths of Britain's Navy is no more?

Have you seen a khaki maggot crawling down a thread of
    cotton—
  the route march of a regiment or so?
Have you seen the narrow riband, unimportant, half-forgotten,
  that tells you that the Thames is far below?
Have you glanced with smiling pity at the world's most famous
    city,
  a large grey smudge that barely strikes the eye?
Would you like to see things truly and appreciate them duly?
  Well then do it, damn you, do it; learn to fly!

Have you left the ground in murkiness all clammy, grey and
    soaking,
  and struggled through the dripping, dirty white?
Have you seen the blank sides closing in and felt that you were
    choking,
  and then leapt into a land of blazing light,
where the burnished sun is shining on the cloud's bright silver
    lining,
  a land where none but fairy feet have trod,
where the splendour nearly blinds you and the wonder of it
    binds you,
  and you know you are in heaven, close to God?

Have you tumbled from the sky until your cries were shrilly
    screaming,
  and watched the earth go spinning round about?
Have you felt the hard air beat your face until your eyes were
    streaming?
  Have you turned the solar system inside out?
Have you seen earth rush to meet you and the fields spread out
    to greet you,
  and flung them back to have another try?

Would it fill you with elation to be boss of all creation?
  Well then do it, damn you, do it; learn to fly!

Have you fought a dummy battle, diving, twisting, pirouetting,
  at a lightning speed that takes away your breath?
Have you been so wildly thrilled that you have found yourself
    forgetting
  that it's practice, not a battle to the death?
Have you hurtled low through narrow, tree-girt spaces like an
    arrow—
  seen things grow and disappear like pricked balloons?
Would you feel the breathless joys of it and hear the thrilling
    noise of it,
  the swish, the roar, the ever-changing tunes?

Have you chased a golden sunbeam down a gold and silver
    alley,
  with pink and orange jewels on the floor?
Have you raced a baby rainbow round a blue and silver valley,
  where purple caves throw back the engine's roar?
Have you seen the lights that smoulder on a cloud's resplendent
    shoulder
  standing out before a saffron-coloured sky?
Would you be in splendid places and illimitable spaces?
  Well then do it, damn you, do it; learn to fly!

JEFFERY DAY

I may not ever have the aeroplane of which I dream, my own
'plane which will be stowed away in a lonely barn between a
hay-tedder and a horse-rake. When I do own it, I shall neglect
it for weeks at a time, but then one morning when there are big
white clouds and the spring air is soft, I shall walk across the
fields and unlock the barn door, and there the 'plane will be
waiting for me. As I edge round it, a brown hen will fly up

cackling from her clutch of eggs in the cockpit and I shall chase her away angrily. There will be a thick layer of hay dust over everything, sparrows will have dropped straws from their nests and have made messes on the wings.

I shall prop open the double doors and lifting the machine by the tail push her out into the sunlight to look her over carefully. Then I shall swing out the wings and lock them, unhook and fold away the jury-struts and kick the chocks into place under the wheels. Then, after flooding the carburettor, turn the prop. over once or twice to suck in, switch on, and seizing the propeller blade, give her one good swing.

As I jolt along, taxiing out into the sixteen acre field, I shall be all alone. There will be no one within sight, not one living thing to watch me and nothing in the sky except a lark or two. And then, when I have strapped myself in and turned into the wind, I shall take-off alone and unobserved into the empty sky.

That is still a dream, and unless it comes true I shall go on, all my life hanging about an aerodrome, flying school machines when I can afford to, gossiping with the ground engineer, and finding pleasure merely in looking at aeroplanes and in watching other people land. I think even if I were to go blind, I should still go to the aerodrome, for the sound of a machine landing thrills me. That bucketting hollow noise that dies into a rumble: as though an empty barrel were bouncing down three stairs and tiptupping to rest: Gosh, it is the most exciting sound I know.

DAVID GARNETT—*A Rabbit in the Air*

THE FLYING FLEA

My daily life is changed. I see everything from another angle. A draught, a journey, an engine starting, a bee buzzing against a pane . . . all these remind me of my aviation.

Life is finer and simpler. My will is freer. I appreciate everything more, sunlight and shade, work and my friends. The sky is vaster. I breathe deep gulps of the fine clear air of the heights. I feel myself to have achieved a higher state of physical strength and a clearer brain. I am living in the third dimension!

Is the weather fit for flying today? The thought makes me look up where ordinary mortals look down. I tap the barometer twenty times a day, and harder when it is going down in the hopes that it will go up!

In dirty weather when I cannot go out I love to take out my maps, spread them on the dining table, put weights on the corners and work out some more aerial voyages. Don't they look pretty with all their little villages and woods? But I know that I am a bad navigator.

Here is a little field between a wood, a marsh, and the railroad; I came down there with a broken petrol tap. Look at that valley! how beautiful it was in the red glow of the setting sun last summer.

When I am walking, motoring, or in the train I look at the country only from one point of view—is it good for landing or not! What a fine smooth meadow, a little small perhaps but with good approaches!

H. MIGNET—The Flying Flea

AMATEUR ADVENTURE

Preface No. 1

The sunshine of today is bright,
Life's morning mists are past,
And visions of a great delight
Are here and mine at last.
The eye is clear, the body strong,
It ripples in the sun,
And life is bursting into song,
For I am twenty-one.

I know it will not last for long
But I am twenty-one.

. . . .

Then roaring down the corridors of space
I will be still, and watch the world go by,
Till dull, known fields and cities of my race
Merge to grey dimness in a dim grey sky.

East to the dawn, and southward to the sun,
Borne on aloft by man's great gift of wings
To legend lands that make the pulses run
And towns that leap with names of ancient kings.

Remote, beyond the mosques of Old Stamboul,
Are wastes, men say, that have a magic still,
Where night winds range the desert, breathing cool,
Slow life on blinded eye and brain and will.

The gods of old looked down beneath their feet
And pitied men. So from the upper air
I will behold the dust, the gasping heat
And know that men have fought and suffered there;

Have cursed the sun and staggered up those wide,
Unending rolls of sand on rolling sand,
Until I drop in the cool eventide
Down to Bokhara, Basra, Samarkand.

. . .

To leave a ghostly, tree-clad Eastern shore,
Dark with a dawn that has not yet begun,
To fly the course that none have flown before,
Across a world of sea to find the sun.

To climb a blueing heaven, height on height,
To see the ocean open wide and grow
Vaster, unbounded save by failing sight—
The ocean that the ships can never know,

That will be life. To feel the engines' power,
Their brave, strong purr, to reach at last the crest
Of my lone island in the sunset hour,
And dipping down the dusk to come to rest.

K. C. GANDAR DOWER—*Amateur Adventure*

AVIATOR—AGED 6

Intent he sat upon an upturned jar,
In youthful disregard of body's ease,
A broken bean pole was his rudder bar,
The stick a cricket stump between his knees,
The plane a battered plank: and laid a-top
Were slips of wood just at the wing-end's tail.
'Those are the ailerons,' quoth he. The prop.
(A piece of driftwood) lolled upon a nail.

  'You must keep flying speed,' he gravely said,
  'And if the engine stops when you take off
  Never turn back or you will soon be dead.'
  And words unspoken warned me not to scoff.

       .   .   .

The summer sun lit up his golden head.
His ears were large and ludicrously spread.

       .   .   .

Will he thus seriously occupy
The cockpit of a squat metallic scout,
And turn that same blue gaze upon the sky,
Straining from cloud to sun and then about
To watch the tail? Will quiet English fields
Reel in the crazy combat round his head
And rattling guns trace out a smoky line
To mark for him the living from the dead?
Will earth receive him star-like in his fires
Or spinning, lifeless, deaf to strumming wires?

RAYMOND WOOD—*Popular Flying*

THE AIRMAN'S ALPHABET

ACE   Pride of parents
and photographed person
and laughter in leather.

BOMB   Curse from cloud
and coming to crook
and saddest to steeple.

COCKPIT   Soft Seat
and support of soldier
and hold for hero.

DEATH   Award for wildness
and worst in the west
and painful to pilots.

ENGINE   Darling of designers
and dirty dragon
and revolving roarer.

FLYING   Habit of hawks
and unholy hunting
and ghostly journey.

GAUGE   Informer about oil
and important to eye
and graduated glass.

HANGAR   Mansion of machine
and motherly to metal
and house of handshaking.

INSTRUMENT Dial on dashboard
and destroyer of doubt
and father of fact.

JOYSTICK   Pivot of power
and responder to pressure
and grip for the glove.

KISS	Touch taking off and tenderness in time and firmness on flesh.
LOOPING	Flying folly and feat at fairs and brave to boys.
MECHANIC	Owner of overalls and interested in iron and trusted with tools.
NOSE-DIVE	Nightmare to nerves and needed by no-one and dash toward death.
OBSERVER	Peeper through periscope and peerer at pasture and eye in the air.
PROPELLER	Wooden wind-oar and twisted whirler and lifter of load.
QUIET	Absent from airmen and easy to horses and got in the grave.
RUDDER	Deflector of flight and flexible fin and pointer of path.
STORM	Night from the north and numbness nearing and hail ahead.
TIME	Expression of alarm and used by the ill and personal space.
UNDER-CARRIAGE	Softener of shock and seat on the soil and easy to injure.

VICTIM   Corpse after crash
and carried through country
and atonement for aircraft.

WIRELESS   Sender of signal
and speaker of sorrow
and news from nowhere.

X   Mark upon map
and meaning mischief
and lover's lingo.

YOUTH   Daydream of devils
and dear to the damned
and always to us.

ZERO   Love before leaving
and touch of terror
and time of attack.

Three signs of an airman—practical jokes—nervousness before taking off—rapid healing after injury.

W. H. AUDEN—*The Orators*

VI
In Full Flight

IN FULL FLIGHT

'En plein vol. . . . Plus haut, toujours plus haut, plus loin,
plus loin toujours.'

BERNARD LAFONT

Lo! these from East, West, South and North,
Swift as a vision issue forth,
Searching the wide ways of the air,
Seeking to lay the secrets bare
Of the wild winds, burning to be
At the heart of heaven's mystery,
In full flight soaring to the skies,
And to heights hid from earthmen's eyes.

I see the shining of their wings,
As of pure immaterial things
Touched with strange beauty in the height,
Or fading now into the night,
And in the light and in the dark,
Still standing for an unseen mark,
Still pressing ever on and on
Where thronging hosts before have gone.

Soon into sudden song they break,
And tones of a wild beauty take;
Like spirits speaking a new tongue
On high I hear in rapture sung
Strains of grave mode, remote and strange,
Such as man dreamed not in the range
Of his dull ears, that he should hear,
The sound of wings as it were near
The gates of heaven, as it were
An host of harpers harping there.
He did not deem that in these days
He should attain the upper ways,

153

That having scoured the ends of earth
He should behold, as at the birth,
This strange new thing, that to the height
He should be borne in solemn flight;
That he should leave the level ground
And in the midst of heaven be found,
Like immortals free to roam
At ease beneath the starry dome.

E. VINE HALL

THE FIRST NON-STOP FLIGHT ACROSS THE ATLANTIC

By Captain John Alcock, D.S.C., and Lieutenant A. Whitten Brown, R.A.F., 14th–15th June 1919

Mr. Winston Churchill, then Secretary of State for War, speaking at a Luncheon given in the Airmen's honour, said:

'In 1492 Christopher Columbus sailed across the Atlantic and discovered America. I cannot help feeling that this afternoon we are to some extent in contact with that event, and that when we welcome our guests, the heroes of today, who have come back from the other side, come to us from America in something less than 16 hours—we are in the presence of another event of something like the same order as that stupendous event which revealed to Europe and Asia the boundless glories and possibilities of the new world across the Atlantic Ocean. How different were those two voyages in all except two conditions—the peril and the pluck: otherwise the difference presents the most violent contrast that could be imagined. In the case of Columbus it occupied 90 days to traverse that immense expanse of waters, and our guests today have come back across the ocean in less than 16 hours; but into those 16 hours were crammed the concentrated perils which required the same great human qualities as were exhibited in that long earlier voyage of ancient times.

154

It is more than 400 years since Columbus discovered America, it is only 10 since Blériot flew the Channel. . . . Think of the broad Atlantic, that terrible waste of desolate waters, tossing in tumult in repeated and almost ceaseless storms, and shrouded with an unbroken canopy of mist. Across this waste, and through this obscurity, two human beings, hurtling through the air, piercing the cloud and darkness, finding their unerring path in spite of every difficulty to their exact objective across those hundreds of miles, arriving almost on schedule time, and at every moment in this voyage liable to destruction from a drop of water in the carburettor, or a spot of oil in their plugs, or a tiny grain of dirt in their feed pipe, or from any of the other hundred and one indirect causes which, in the present state of aeronautics, might drag an aeroplane to its fate.

When one considers all these factors I really do not know what we should admire the most in our guests—their audacity, their determination, their skill, their science, their Vimy-Vickers aeroplane, their Rolls-Royce engines, or their good fortune. All these were necessary and all of them contributed to their achievement, and to the event which brought us all together here this afternoon, to cheer the victors of the first non-stop Atlantic Flight.

(During the luncheon Mr. Churchill announced that His Majesty the King had assented to the award of the Knight-Commandership of the Order of the British Empire to both Captain Alcock and Lieutenant Brown.)

THE DESERT MAIL

(Cairo—Baghdad, 1922)

Clean cut against the first faint flush of dawn,
  Their silver planes outstretched to catch the sun,

Hastening to meet the Day as yet unborn,
　　Faint upon the earth their engines' muted hum.
Below—the Desert lies in shadow dim,
　　A vast, inverted bowl of yellow sand.
The distant hills, eternal guardians grim,
　　Flanking the entrance to a barren land.

　　　　For His Majesty's Mails are travelling East,
　　　　　　(Mark the Track as it winds below.)
　　　　His Majesty's Mails are travelling East,
　　　　　　(Six hundred weary miles to go!)

The ashes of a fire—lit all in vain—
　　A Thing that breathed and lived but yesterday,
The charred and blackened wreckage of a 'plane,
　　Are all that mark the Man Who Lost his Way.
An error of a minute; a side-slip in a cloud;
　　He failed to see the Track he thought he knew,
Then endless days of waiting—by fear and hunger cowed—
　　Ere the jackals took the meat that was their due!

　　　　For His Majesty's Mails are travelling East,
　　　　　　(The Track is dim in the sand below.)
　　　　His Majesty's Mails are travelling East.
　　　　　　(Only two hundred miles to go!)

In the bitter cold of Winter, when the sullen engines fret,
　　And the leaden sky above them bids them stay,
In the storm or in the sunshine; in the dry or in the wet,
　　The Air Mail passes swiftly on its way.
In the hottest days of Summer, when the water-holes are dry,
　　And the Desert's full of things that are not there,
The gaunt and weary jackal sees the shadows passing by
　　Of the Mail 'planes as they hurry through the air.

　　　　For His Majesty's Mails are travelling East.
　　　　　　(The Arrow is pointing the way to go.)

His Majesty's Mails are travelling East.
(Those are the Bitumen Pools below.)

We have placed at your disposal all the arts we learnt in War,
  And for ninepence you can purchase, if you're wise,
The same efficient service of the Man who Yesterday,
  Chased the black-crossed Birds of War from out your skies.
The letters that they carry from Cairo to the East,
  Bear little slips of paper, coloured blue,
And the loss of crew and pilot doesn't matter in the least,
  If the Mail Bags see the Desert journey through!

For His Majesty's Mails are travelling East.
(The Track is lost but the way we know.)
His Majesty's Mails are travelling East.
(Baghdad City to port below!)

J. O. P. E.—*The Aeroplane*

LINKING THE NEW WORLD WITH THE OLD

Across the Atlantic—East to West

. . . The flight obviously must be attempted during the summer months, for the weather during the winter was impossible to conquer with existing equipment (this was in 1933). The machine was a special job and took months to construct. At last it was ready, and a take-off was attempted. Paper figures let us down, and the under-carriage refused to stand up to the terrific strain imposed upon it. The plane went back for repairs and for strengthening of the 'under-cart'.

Next came a wait of many weary weeks for suitable weather conditions. Without wireless, we dared not risk leaving unless we knew that conditions were reasonably stable. Moreover, as we were flying east to west, against the prevailing winds, we dared not take off if the winds were stronger than an average of

20 m.p.h. against us, as we should not have had enough petrol to reach the other side.

At last came a report the winds were light and variable. Low cloud and mist were prevalent but we were most vitally concerned with the winds. We decided to take off. Would the under-carriage stand up to it this time? Instead of an aerodrome, we had chosen a beach with a seven-mile run over smooth, hard sand. Immediately overhead the sun shone, but ahead were black clouds and fog sheathing the coast-line of Ireland, which should have been our guide for the beginning of the flight.

After a few minutes of tight-held breath we felt the plane lift. Gingerly turning to seek the coast-line, we ran into swirling clouds of mist, spray, and low cloud. Missing a cliff by inches, we climbed carefully and prayerfully, and at last emerged above the clouds into a new world, a wilderness of blue sky staring at a marble floor. Seemingly suspended between the two, we could only judge speed or forward movement by a glance at our air-speed indicator, which showed a speed of 100 m.p.h.

And so we went on; hour after hour after monotonous hour. Only the air-speed told us we were moving, and the passage of the sun over our heads that the day was running its natural course. Of the restless waves of the Atlantic far below us we saw nothing. Nothing happened to break the awful monotony. Our imaginations ran riot. Were our instruments lying? Were we really many hundred miles out to sea? What was below us? The urge to go down and see became well-nigh unconquerable, but common sense came to the rescue and saved us this waste of time and fuel.

The sun sank slowly towards the horizon. It disappeared, leaving us more lonely than before as it took from us its cheerful face, yet leaving behind light enough to fade the friendly, twinkling stars. For we were now very far north, away north of the shipping route, on the fringe of the summer region of perpetual daylight.

Wisps of cloud materialized in front of us and were cut, like so much paper, by our propellers. As though in defiance, the wisps got together, consolidated, until they formed a large angry mass blocking our way. Plunging into its depths, having no alternative, we steadily climbed, eyes glued to flickering luminous figures on our instrument-board—pin-points of light on the accuracy of which our safety depended. Hours and hours passed, with nothing to do but keep the compass on its course and the plane on a level keel. This sounds easy enough, but its very simplicity becomes a danger, when your head keeps nodding with weariness and utter boredom and your eyes everlastingly try to shut out the confusing rows of figures in front of you, which will insist on getting jumbled together. Tired of trying to sort them out, you relax for a second, then your head drops and you sit up with a jerk. Where are you? What are you doing here? Oh, yes, of course, you are somewhere in the middle of the North Atlantic, with hungry waves below you like vultures impatiently waiting for the end.

When a petrol tank runs dry and the propeller falters for a moment, you wake up thoroughly, with fear as the alarm-bell. You know you must let the tank run quite dry before switching on to the next, otherwise you cannot be sure of using every drop of precious fuel, for the gauges are not accurate for the last few gallons. Electric fuel gauges accurate to the last drop are amongst luxuries available today but denied to record-seeking pilots of earlier times.

At last the long-imagined dawn really came. The sky lightened slowly, very slowly, and revealed a scene of lonely desolation, hard to beat. A ceiling of pale sky dropped down to join a white flat floor, for all the world like a giant's pudding-basin clapped upside down on a layer of dough. Like a fly caught inside, we were trapped within its walls, and there seemed no escape, no beginning and no end. We must have faith in something, so, almost against our will, we followed the compass westwards. Suddenly the floor below us was cut away, and we had a funny feeling we were going over the edge of the world. It was only the rim of the cloud layer—in reality, the famed and dreaded Newfoundland fog-banks, over which we had been flying for many hours—and we could now see, for the first time since leaving the coast, the glint of water thousands of feet below. Straining our eyes, we peered into the dim distance in search of land. We saw peculiar vague outlines which looked like small white islands when the sun touched them, and only as we drew nearer did we realize that they were icebergs. Soon the water was littered with lumps of drift-ice, like a huge bath strewn with soap-flakes.

Flying low down, we had a glorious sensation of speed and movement, now that we had objects to flash past our wings and leave behind. If we had not been so tired, we might have reflected on the peculiarities of speed. What is speed anyway? Only the relationship in terms of movement of one object to another. We were too weary to pursue such a will-o'-the-wisp of thought. It was only important to *feel* we were moving—when you are very tired, it is good to have the senses confirm what the brain already knows. Our brain was telling us, too, that we were very near land, but we needed to see it to be convinced. At last we did. Land was there ahead. Bleak, barren and inhospitable. A forced landing on its rocks would have been fully as hopeless as one in the waters below, but it was land, and our senses were satisfied. We had crossed the North Atlantic.

Two thousand miles of water at an average cruising speed, against head-winds, of 80 miles an hour. Today you could cross that ocean in ten hours in four-engined flying-boats. Warmly tucked up in a sleeping-berth, you could go to sleep this side of the Atlantic and open your eyes in the New World—a real new world of which you can be sure, not the ghostly new world which awaited those who failed in the pioneer days.

AMY JOHNSON—*Sky Roads of the World*

FLYING IN THE ANTARCTIC, 1934

Weather is simultaneously the greatest hazard and the greatest obstacle to flying in the polar regions. Most of all it is an obstacle. Day after day of waiting, day after day of intransigeant cloudiness, low stratus clouds packed solidly 500 feet or so overhead, no horizon, just a meaningless fuzzy blue in all directions. Flying in that stuff, I once observed, was like flying in a bowl of milk. Occasionally one gets caught in it on a long flight; but no-one in his right senses would deliberately take off in it. The soft grey rolls of the Barrier melt meaninglessly into the grey roof of the sky; there is nothing to mark the joining; even with a mile visibility, in that suffocated perspective a pilot, flying low, could crash into a hill and never know what hit him. Men running on skis are bewildered and confused by the shapeless aspect of things before them.

And so you wait, hopelessly consulting a sky that seems to be pressing down your temples. The twenty-four hours of daylight make the waiting seem all the longer. You can't imagine how discouraging it is to poke your head out of the hatch, no matter what the hour, and find the world exactly as it has been for days, with no outward evidence of growth or change, no sign of waxing or waning—nothing but an accretion of unprofitable hours. Sometimes a hole will appear, patches of deep blue sky bursting through the grey; and just when your hopes rise the holes will close as rapidly as they appeared. It is amazing how swiftly conditions will change, under certain conditions of wind. I have seen an utterly solid clouded sky dissolve and become crystal clear in less than half an hour, and clear skies become impenetrable masses of black billowy clouds in the same time. That's why, in waiting for a flight, you must be on your toes to seize the break the instant it appears and ram through the flight with all possible dispatch, lest the opportunity vanish entirely or the return be jeopardized by a change for the worse. . . .

Shortly after midnight, November 15th, the break came. . . .

A beautiful day, a perfect day for flying. A fleckless sky, visibility that seemed to run on for ever, and the plane's shadow running ahead of it across the wind-riffled Barrier. Over the smashed and contorted pressure of the Bad Lands in the upper canyon of Amundsen Arm, holding a south-easterly course. All that broad white plain running to the horizon, whiter than any white on earth, and all untrodden, unexplored. . . .

No simple job is navigating a plane in the Antarctic. Just as at sea, there are frequently no conspicuous landmarks with which to check course and direction. But the polar regions give rise to their own peculiar problems. Owing to the proximity of the Magnetic Pole the magnetic compass is unreliable; it is sluggish, reluctant to settle down, subject to wide swings. There is the problem of direction caused by the rapid convergence of meridians toward the Pole. In any direction but due north or south in high southern latitudes a plane flying a straight course cuts rapidly across meridians at quickly changing angles. Thus direction changes constantly: time, too, with the same rapidity, an hour every 180 miles on an easterly or westerly course in Little America's latitude. So between making compensations for changing time and direction, resetting the sun compass, checking drift with the drift-indicator, calculating ground speed, plotting positions and laying new courses, a navigator, in Bill Bowlin's phrase, 'is busier than a barber's cat'. . . .

At 11,000 feet we passed by Mt. Grace McKinley. A bow and beam bearing put us 23 miles east of it and exactly on our course.

From this lofty perch we had a full view of this refrigerated world, a view which, once seen, can never vanish from the mind, but lingers with the unrelaxing clarity of something at

once so terrible and still so beautiful that it impoverishes all
other spectacles. Grey masses of rock that a giant hand might
have strewn about like so many pebbles filled the north-eastern
horizon. Battered, eroded, carved and splintered by an ice sheet
which still drowned all but their highest shoulders and ridges,
they looked what they were, the shattered derelicts of an Ice
Age, the remnants of the land which had stood off the warring
assault of the ice.

REAR ADMIRAL R. E. BYRD—Antarctic Discovery

ENGLAND TO AUSTRALIA

Sing we the two lieutenants, Parer and M'Intosh,
After the War wishing to hie them home to Australia,
Planned they would take a high way, a hazardous, crazy air-
    way:
Death their foregone conclusion, a flight headlong to failure,
We said. For no silver posh
Plane was their pigeon, no dandy dancer quick-stepping
    through heaven,
But a craft of obsolete design, a condemned D.H. nine;
Sold for a song it was, patched up though to write an heroic
Line across the world as it reeled on its obstinate stoic
Course to that southern haven.

On January 8, 1920, their curveting wheels kissed
England good-bye. Over Hounslow huddled in morning mist
They rose and circled like buzzards while we rubbed our sleepy
    eyes:
Like a bird scarce-fledged they flew, whose flying hours are
    few—
Still dear is the nest but deeper its desire unto the skies—
And they left us to our sleeping.
They felt earth's warning tug on their wings: vain to advance
Asking a thoroughfare through the angers of the air

On so flimsy a frame: but they pulled up her nose and the earth
    went sloping
Away, and they aimed for France.

Fog first, a wet blanket, a kill-joy, the primrose-of-morning's
    blight,
Blotting out the dimpled sea, the ample welcome of land,
The gay glance from the bright
Cliff-face behind, snaring the sky with treachery, sneering
At hope's loss of height. But they charged it, flying blind;
They took a compass-bearing against that dealer of doubt,
As a saint when the field of vision is fogged gloriously steels
His spirit against the tainter of air, the elusive taunter:
They climbed to win a way out,
Then downward dared till the moody waves snarled at their
    wheels.

Landing at last near Conteville, who had skimmed the crest
    of oblivion,
They could not rest, but rose and flew on to Paris, and there
Trivially were delayed—a defective petrol feed—
Three days: a time hung heavy on
Hand and heart, till they leapt again to the upper air,
Their element, their lover, their angel antagonist.
Would have taken a fall without fame, but the sinewy
    framework the wrist
Of steel the panting engine wrestled well: and they went
South while the going was good, as a swallow that guide nor
    goad
Needs on his sunny scent.

At Lyons the petrol failed again, and forty-eight hours
They chafed to be off, the haughty champions whose breathing-
    space
Was an horizon span and the four winds their fan.

Over Italy's shores
A reverse, the oil ran out and cursing they turned about
Losing a hundred miles to find a landing-place.
Not a coast for a castaway this, no even chance of alighting
On sward or wind-smooth sand:
A hundred miles without pressure they flew, the engine
     fighting
For breath, and its heart nearly burst before they dropped to
     land.

And now the earth they had spurned rose up against them in
     anger,
Tier upon tier it towered, the terrible Apennines:
No sanctuary there for wings, no flares nor landing-lines,
No hope of floor and hangar.
Yet those ice-tipped spears that disputed the passage set spurs
To their two-hundred and forty horsepower; grimly they
     gained
Altitude, though the hand of heaven was heavy upon them,
The downdraught from the mountains: though desperate
     eddies spun them
Like a coin, yet unkindly tossed their luck came uppermost
And mastery remained.

Air was all ambushes round them, was avalanche earthquake
Quicksand, a funnel deep as doom, till climbing steep
They crawled like a fly up the face of perpendicular night
And levelled, finding a break
At fourteen thousand feet. Here earth is shorn from sight:
Deadweight a darkness hangs on their eyelids, and they bruise
Their eyes against a void: vindictive the cold airs close
Down like a trap of steel and numb them from head to heel;
Yet they kept an even keel,
For their spirit reached forward and took the controls while
     their fingers froze.

They had not heard the last of death. When the mountains were
    passed,
He raised another crest, the long crescendo of pain
Kindled to climax, the plane
Took fire. Alone in the sky with the breath of their enemy
Hot in their face they fought: from three thousand feet they
    tilted
Over, side-slipped away—a trick for an ace, a race
And running duel with death: flame streamed out behind,
A crimson scarf of, as life-blood out of a wound, but the wind
Of their downfall staunched it; death wilted,
Lagged and died out in smoke—he could not stay their pace.

A lull for a while. The powers of hell rallied their legions.
On Parer now fell the stress of the flight; for the plane had been
    bumped,
Buffeted, thrashed by the air almost beyond repair;
But he tinkered and he coaxed, and they limped
Over the Adriatic on into warmer regions.
Erratic their course to Athens, to Crete: coolly they rode her
Like a tired horse at the water-jumps, they jockeyed her over seas,
Till they came at last to a land whose dynasties of sand
Had seen Alexander, Napoleon, many a straddling invader,
But never none like these.

England to Cairo, a joy-ride, a forty-hour journey at most,
Had cost them forty-four days. What centuried strata of life
Fuelled the fire that haled them to heaven, the power that held
    them
Aloft? For their plane was a laugh,
A patch, brittle as matchstick, a bubble, a lift for a ghost:
Bolts always working loose of propeller, cylinder, bearer;
Instruments faulty; filter, magneto, each strut unsound.
Yet after four days, though we swore she never could leave the
    ground,

We saw her in headstrong haste diminish towards the east—
That makeshift, mad sky-farer.

Aimed they now for Baghdad, unwritten in air's annals
A voyage. But theirs the fate all flights of logic to refute,
Who obeyed no average law, who buoyed the viewless
    channels
Of sky with a courage steadfast, luminous. Safe they crossed
Sinai's desert, and daring
The Nejd, the unneighbourly waste of Arabia, yet higher
    soaring
(Final a fall there for birds of passage, limed and lost
In shifty the sand's embrace) all day they strove to climb
Through stormy rain: but they felt her shorten her stride and
    falter,
And they fell at evening time.

Slept that night beside their machine, and the next morning
Raider Arabs appeared reckoning this stranded bird
A gift: like cobras they struck, and their gliding shadows
    athwart
The sand were all their warning.
But the aeronauts, knowing iron the coinage here, had brought
Mills bombs and revolvers, and M'Intosh held them off
While Parer fought for life—
A spark, the mechanic's right answer, and finally wrought
A miracle, for the dumb engine spoke and they rose
Convulsively out of the clutch of the desert, the clench of their
    foes.

Orchestrate this theme, artificer-poet. Imagine
The roll, crackling percussion, quickening tempo of engine
For a start: the sound as they soar, an octave-upward slur
Scale of sky ascending:
Hours-held note of level flight, a beat unhurried,
Sustaining undertone of movement never-ending:

Wind shrill on the ailerons, flutes and fifes in a flurry
Devilish when they dive, plucking of tense stays.
These hardly heard it, who were the voice, the heavenly air
That sings above always.

We have seen the extremes, the burning, the freezing, the
    outward face
Of their exploit; heroic peaks, tumbling-to-zero depressions:
Little our graph can show, the line they traced through space,
Of the heart's passionate patience.
How soft drifts of sleep piled on their senses deep
And they dug themselves out often: how the plane was a weight
    that hung
And swung on their aching nerve; how din drilled through the
    skull
And sight sickened—so slow earth filtered past below.
Yet nerve failed never, heart clung
To height, and the brain kept its course and the hand its skill.

Baghdad renewed a propeller damaged in desert. Arid
Baluchistan spared them that brought down and spoilt with
    thirst
Armies of Alexander. To Karachi they were carried
On cloud-back: fragile as tinder their plane, but the winds were
    tender
Now to their need, and nursed
Them along till teeming India made room for them to alight.
Wilting her wings, the sweltering suns had moulted her bright
Plumage, rotten with rain
The fabric: but they packed her with iron washers and tacked
    her
Together, good for an hour, and took the air again.

Feats for a hundred flights, they were prodigal of: a fairest
Now to tell—how they foiled death when the engine failed
Above the Irrawaddy, over close-woven forest.

What shoals for a pilot there, what a snarled passage and dark
Shelves down to doom and grip
Of green! But look, balanced superbly, quick off the mark
Swooping like centre three-quarter whose impetus storms a
    gap—
Defenders routed, rooted their feet, and their arms are mown
Aside, that high or low aim at his overthrow—
M'Intosh touched her down.

And they picked her up out of it somehow and put her at the
    air, a
Sorry hack for such steeplechasing, to leap the sky.
'We'll fly this bloody crate till it falls to bits at our feet,'
Said the mechanic Parer.
And at Moulmein soon they crashed; and the plane by their
    spirit's high
Tension long pinned, girded and guarded from dissolution,
Fell to bits at their feet. Wrecked was the under-carriage,
Radiator cracked, in pieces, compasses crocked;
Fallen all to confusion.
Their winged hope was a heap of scrap, but unsplintered their
    courage.

Six weeks they worked in sun-glare and jungle damps,
    assembling
Fragments to make airworthy what was worth not its weight
    in air.
As a surgeon, grafter of skin, as a setter of bones tumbling
Apart, they had power to repair
This good for naught but the grave: they livened her engine and
    gave
Fuselage faith to rise rejuvenated from ruin.
Went with them stowaways, not knowing what hazard they
    flew in—
Bear-cubs, a baby alligator, lizards and snakes galore;

Mascots maybe, for the plane though twice she was floored
again
Always came up for more.

Till they came to the pitless mountains of Timor. Yet these,
untamed,
Not timorous, against the gradient and Niagara of air they
climbed
Scarce-skimming the summits; and over the shark-toothed
Timor sea
Lost their bearings, but shirked not the odds, the deaths that
lurked
A million to one on their trail:
They reached out to the horizon and plucked their destiny.
On for eight hours they flew blindfold against the unknown,
And the oil began to fail
And their flying spirit waned—one pint of petrol remained
When the land stood up to meet them and they came into their
own.

Southward still to Melbourne, the bourn of their flight, they
pressed
Till at last near Culcairn, like a last fretted leaf
Falling from brave autumn into earth's breast,
D.H. nine, their friend that had seen them to the end,
Gave up her airy life.
The Southern Cross was splendid above the spot where she
fell,
The end of her rainbow curve over our weeping day:
And the flyers, glad to be home, unharmed by that dizzy fall,
Dazed as the dead awoken from death, stepped out of the
broken
Body and went away.

What happened then, the roar
and rave of waving crowds

That fêted them, was only
   an afterglow of glory
Reflected on the clouds
   where they had climbed alone,
Day's golden epilogue :
   and them, whose meteor path
Lightened our eyes, whose great
   spirit lifted the fog
That sours a doubtful earth,
   the stars commemorate.

        Cecil Day Lewis—*A Time to Dance*

OVER EVEREST

. . . We were now in the strong westerly wind and continued to climb steadily, heading well to the left of Everest. As we rose the table became smaller and more peaks appeared over the far side until at last we were looking down on the whole of the table-top which stretched to all horizons and all the Himalayas above 19,000 ft. were sticking through its surfaces. The altimeter showed 30,000 ft. and we calculated that we must be somewhere over Komaltar, the point in the Arun Valley, which was to have been the start of our survey. However, it was impossible to see down through the haze and we had to make a rough guess at the starting-place and hope that the filters on the lenses of the vertical cameras would penetrate the dust.

Clydesdale's aircraft appeared to be climbing more easily than mine. The slower climb of the Wallace was probably due to its extra load represented by Bonnett's heavy cinema cameras and film. I was being gradually left behind and below. Everest loomed closer and as we passed to the right of Chamlang it appeared to tower above us. We began to realize that we should have started to climb seriously earlier in the flight, but we reckoned we could still clear the summit by perhaps 1,000 ft.

The wind was obviously much stronger than we had been told, the plume from Everest was streaking along the 12 miles range to Makalu at hurricane force.

As we moved on towards Lhotse, the southernmost peak of the Everest group, I noticed that something extraordinary was happening. The machine appeared to be climbing as well as ever, the engine was giving full power, yet we were being slowly blown down on to the westerly slopes of Makalu. A moment before its summit had been well below us; now it was towering a good thousand feet above. A hasty glance at the altimeter showed a steady decrease in height where there should have been a steady increase. The temptation was to try and climb faster which was impossible and would have resulted in a stall into the base of Lhotse.

We were in a tremendous down-rush of air. Though the machine continued to climb, it was climbing in an air current that was carrying it down at a much greater velocity. Two thousand feet were lost before the down-rush cushioned itself out on the glacier beds. We were in a most serious position. The great bulk of Everest was towering above us to the left, Makalu down-wind to the right and the connecting range dead ahead, with a hurricane wind doing its best to carry us over and dash us on the knife-edge sides of Makalu. I had the feeling we were hemmed in on all sides, and that we dare not turn away to gain height afresh. There was plenty of air-space behind us, yet it was impossible to turn back. A turn to the left meant going back into the down-current and the peaks below; a turn down-wind to the right would have taken us almost instantly into Makalu at 200 miles an hour.

There was nothing we could do but climb straight ahead and hope to clear the lowest point in the barrier range. The machine was almost at its ceiling, apt to be sloppy on the controls, and the slightest error in flying would have meant a fatal loss of height. With the aircraft heading almost straight into the wind, we crabbed sideways towards the ridge, unable to determine if we were level with it or below. A fortunate up-current just short of the ridge carried us up a few feet and we scraped over. The North-East ridge appeared to sweep up vertically from our port-wings to the summit, and we could see straight down the sheer north side to the glacier cradles at the base of Everest. We were still far short of our objective.

Then started a grim fight for height. We had to turn very carefully towards Everest and then back over the ridge again with the little height we had gained and face the same fight over again. This business of turning towards the edge of a down-draught in order to climb seems even in retrospect a mad risk. At the time it was very much like a nightmare. The mind was obsessed by the knowledge that we must avoid being blown back on Makalu and yet must approach dangerously close to it in order to have sufficient space for a slow, gentle turn to the right without being caught in the down-rush. The invisible menace of the down-draught had all the qualities of a nightmare. One had to try and imagine its limits and position from the topography.

Straight ahead lay safety which is unnaturally attractive and tempting to a mind weakened with lack of oxygen and low atmospheric pressure. The sense of responsibility for one's passenger in such a case threatens to overset all reason. An abnormal effort was required to make the decision and risk that turn towards the unseen down-rush, and then crab over the ridge once more. Three times we had to repeat this performance, gaining a little height each time, until we reckoned we had sufficient height to venture round the north side and over the top of Everest.

All this time Bonnett was working hard with his cameras, making the most of the quite remarkable opportunities afforded by this close encounter with the mountain. I often wonder whether Bonnett fully appreciated the seriousness of our situation during these manoeuvres. We have never discussed it, but it is almost unbelievable that a man could carry on working his cameras while the highest mountain in the world seemed to rush straight at him if he had any doubts about the machine's ability to clear it. This coolness was to save his life within the next few moments.

As we swept round to the north side of Everest and swung left to come over the top, Bonnett went below to fill his camera with film for the summit. While he crouched down in the cockpit he unfortunately trod on his oxygen feed-pipe and on rising, pulled and fractured the pipe close to the mask. The first he knew about it was that he had weakened and could no longer support the weight of his camera. He sank on to the floor and with his remaining consciousness, checked over the oxygen flow and its heating apparatus. Finding nothing wrong there, he felt for a leakage, found the fracture and bound a handkerchief over the break. He made another vain attempt to struggle up into the slipstream with his camera.

The effort used up what little strength was left and he collapsed unconscious on the floor, while I waited for him to appear before going over the top. I had seen him slip below and soon realized that something had happened to him. I decided to go over the top, register the summit on the survey camera and then lose height as quickly as possible. My anxiety about Bonnett was counteracted to some extent by the sight of Clydesdale's machine to the north of the mountain. This was the first I had seen of the other machine since we were separated by the down-rush. As I turned, I saw it clear the top of Everest on a southerly course.

A hurried glance at the summit before it disappeared under the aircraft, showed a tiny platform that appeared to have standing room for about four people. I remember thinking to myself, 'Well, we are over the top, but what a failure from a survey point of view,' and then I suddenly had the sensation of freezing cold around the nose and mouth. I jumped immediately to the conclusion that the oxygen heating had failed. This was serious as it was only a matter of time until the water content would freeze in the valve and stop the flow. Actually, the complete metal nose-piece, carrying the microphone and oxygen feed had dropped from the mask and was lying on my knee. In my anxiety for Bonnett, I had no doubt turned my head too far round and dragged the nose-piece away from the mask. I quickly tried to get it back in position and refix it, but found this impossible with heavy gloves. I was compelled to hold it in place.

The first 60 miles of the return flight proved the most unpleasant I have ever experienced. Throughout that long half-hour I was holding the oxygen feed against the mask with one hand and with the other flying the aircraft, regulating engine temperature, oxygen flow and altitude boost control. I was worried about Bonnett lying unconscious or dead in the rear cockpit, and was tempted to lose height faster than was safe to see if the figure of Bonnett would come to life with the decrease in altitude. Not a movement until we were over Forbesganj at 8,000 ft., and by that time I had given up all hope.

Then a reflection in the windscreen or some less tangible sense of movement attracted my attention and made me look round once more. To my intense relief, Bonnett was struggling up from the floor, tearing off mask and headgear. He was a nasty dark green shade but obviously alive and that was enough for the moment. Twenty minutes later we were circling the familiar landing ground at Lalbalu, canvas hangars, swimming pool and all. By the time we had landed, all our troubles seemed to have happened weeks ago, were almost forgotten and we were able to cope with the greetings and questions in a cool and collected manner. All I had to show for the swift and harassing troubles of that flight was a blister on the back of my hand where a heating element in the glove had done its work a bit too well. Bonnett emerged a little shyly with his damaged oxygen pipe and at my suggestion the doctor had a look at him. Beyond that we said nothing about the trials that had seemed so tremendous at 30,000 ft. above.

Flight-Lieutenant D. F. M'Intyre—*The Pilots' Book of Everest*

A CLIMB IN A CLOUD

Sailplaning in Excelsis, 8th June 1938

High flying in sailplanes is perhaps the final development of the art of motorless flight, and requires a training and technique additional to all that the pilot has learnt before in achieving, first, duration, then thermal and distance flying. This is because above a certain height most climbs must be made flying blind in unstable clouds, and it is unfortunate that blind flying training, which is done in aeroplanes, as well as the special instruments and parachute necessary to reduce the hazards inseparable from the rough conditions likely to be encountered, are expensive. This is the reason why so few high flights have hitherto been made in this country.

The main difficulty of flying blind is that the pilot is subject to attacks of extreme vertigo, brought on either by very rough conditions or, in the case of sailplane pilots, by the need to fly blind in constant circles in order to remain within the areas of rising air which are found inside the right kinds of clouds. . . .

The strength factors of the Minimoa are much greater than those of a fighting aeroplane. To assist him the pilot has certain instruments, and he must learn to obey these while his senses are peremptorily telling him to do the very reverse: and fortunately, after a few lessons under a hood in a two-seater aeroplane, one does in fact learn to divorce one's actions from one's instincts, though this partial immunity is temporary and has to be renewed regularly every year, or more often if necessary. But there is a great deal to be learnt about the internal gust-structure of unstable clouds, so that flying to great heights is still something of an adventure.

One Sunday I took off from the site of the London Gliding Club on Dunstable Downs at 3 p.m. The conditions were good, but not extremely so, and I had no idea of going for a height record. At about 4.30, however, I struck a strong up-current, and, in company wth a friend in another machine, circled up to near the base of a small cloud over Luton, at about 4,500 feet. From here I could see a rather large storm-cloud building up over Leighton Buzzard, some 8 miles to the west so flew towards this. As I got nearer, it became clear that there was a very active current of air ascending into it. The base looked quite flat, as is the case with nearly all active cumulus clouds, except that along the far edge there seemed to be a darker slate-grey area, denoting a greater depth of cloud-vapour above, bordered by a hanging ragged fringe which could be seen to form constantly and to be constantly ascending into the cloud above. As I approached this, my rate-of-climb indicator showed increasing lift, until it moved up to a speed of 10 feet a second. I put the machine into a circle and spiralled rapidly upwards. At this point the rapid upcurrent of air had lifted the seemingly flat ceiling of cloud somewhat, so that I spiralled up into a kind of diving bell, the walls formed of blue-grey cloud, with below a reducing circle of sunlit green fields. The base of this bell sank slowly down. We approached the ceiling, and everything vanished. The time when I went into the cloud was 5.10 p.m., the height about 4,900 feet.

Entering a big cloud in a sailplane is a very different experience from doing the same thing in an aeroplane, for in the powered craft the general noise and vibration overshadow the subtler flavours of flight. I had the feeling that we had been suddenly absorbed by a large and immensely powerful octopus. The rush of air over the wings and body of the machine took on a different key and became smoother and quieter. One felt as though entrapped in an envelope of sticky powder. The hue of the surrounding vapour, a bluish-black, was octopus-like too. This, of course, was due to the great thickness of the cloud at this point, for I subsequently discovered it was more than a mile high. It is only the shallower clouds or the fringes of the big ones which assume the friendly hues of white or light grey.

The rate of climb now gradually increased to 15 feet a second, the only sound being the comforting buzz of the little electric motor of my twin indicator. For a while the air rose smoothly and swiftly, then we struck a rough area, and the machine started to lurch. Simultaneously I began to feel marked vertigo, my head started to swim, and my senses to convey impressions quite different from those recorded by my instruments. Before going into the cloud I had noticed that the edge nearest to my point of entry lay to the north, so I now straightened the machine from its right-hand circles (which operation gave me the most violent, but false, impression of doing a steep left-hand climbing turn), and held her rather grimly on a northerly compass course, which about 5 minutes later brought us out of the towering wall of dazzling cloud into the sunlight at 7,500 feet. I flew around, losing height, for a few minutes until the vertigo had subsided, then headed back into the cloud. My intention was to fly straight through it and out the other side, but after first negotiating a very violent down-current, which shot me down at nearly 20 feet a second, I struck a smooth patch of air rising nearly as fast, so again put my machine into a circle and climbed very fast indeed.

Now ice started to form on all protuberances, on the front of the cockpit cover and the leading edge of the wings. However, I did not meet any rain or hail, which is usual in such clouds, and I knew that Minimoas had emerged successfully from much more severe conditions after cloud flights in Germany, and was not worried. But the nervous strain is considerable for the amateur and it was with some relief I saw the needle of my altimeter at last top 10,000 feet which was the height I had set myself to reach. I straightened up again and steered a southerly course. The surrounding cloud gradually lightened, then a gap appeared ahead. With joy I anticipated seeing the earth again. But I was disappointed. I came out of my cloud to find far beneath me apparently stretching in all directions the bulging tops of an unbroken sea of cumulus. Behind me, a mountain of white rising out of the white plain beneath, my storm-cloud towered yet another 1,500 feet up into the blue sky. It was a sight to dazzle the gods. . . . It was 5.45. I had been 35 minutes inside the cloud. As I slowly descended towards the cloudsheet beneath I searched for a gap through which I might descend without having to do further blind flying with the possibility of encountering more unwanted lift inside the clouds beneath, and at length I did in fact find a small gap through which I could see, an incredible distance below, a vista of green and brown fields and a road. I circled steeply down through this, occasionally penetrating the surrounding cloud and emerged a short while later just to the north of Luton, my cloud having drifted 8 miles while I was inside it.

I set the nose of the Minimoa back west to Dunstable and had a good look round. Along the leading edge of the wing, 58 feet in span, ran a three-quarter-inch ribbon of jagged ice-crystals. Similar crystals had formed on the front of my transparent cockpit-cover and on various protuberances on the outside of the machine. In absolute silence we planed down to 4,000 feet, when a sharp crack made me jump in my seat. I looked anxiously round. Then a spark of watery light flew by, and a lump of ice, melted from the nose, flew back and hit the wing with a crack like splintering wood. Next similar sounds started from the tail, and it was quite a relief when at about 2,000 feet the last white fragments had gone and all was quiet.

The landing was at 6.15, and the height recorded on my barographs, subject to official correction, was rather over 10,000 feet.

PHILIP WILLS—*The Times*

VII
Landscapes and Skyscapes

CLOUD PICTURES

At noon, all weary ashes, the sky is one wan shade,
Till on its bosom flashes a flower many rayed.
In naked splendour turning, it opens on the blue
And soon the South is burning, where sunlight conquers
     through.

The cumuli, in billows, with rounded heads and grey,
Still roll their rainy pillows to smother dying day.
Athwart the gloom advances, with fiery flight in vain,
A sheaf of crimson lances that break and leave no stain.

Above a winter gloaming, with sunset at the leas,
Rode golden galleons homing, upon their purple seas;
And when all light was muted, and shone the after-glow,
Those fairy ships saluted before they sank below.

In vast and patterned order throng cirri round the moon,
To spread their fleecy border for Dian's silver shoon;
And through each cloudy wrinkle—red, blue and violet—
Small stars peep out and twinkle, like fishes in a net.

A day's death still and tender at dusky edge of night
With one faint cloudlet slender, hung in the green owl-light;
And through that peace abiding a rosy flash it flings,
Then stoops, like seraph hiding his head beneath his wings.

EDEN PHILLPOTTS

FROM 'PRELUDE TO ICAROS'

Wings!
Wings heavy over the mountains!
Wings heavy over the coastal and interior plains!
Wings heavier still over the oceans and the tributaries of the
     oceans!

Wings in the darker blue where the hills are not,
where the round white clouds
and the cloud-floors
pass and repass
on their long wanderings,
where storms pile
cloud-mountain on cloud-mountain,
where thunders are,
and the snake-tongues of lightning,
and the hail's hatcheries!

JOHN WILLIAMS ANDREWS—*Prelude to Icaros*

AN ASCENT FROM CHAMBERSBURG
Pa. 1840

. . . My aerial ship entered a dense black body of clouds. . . . When I emerged from this ocean of clouds a new and wonderfully magnificent scene greeted my eyes. . . . The profile of the cloud surface was more depressed than that on the earth, and in the distance of the cloud valley a magnificent sight presented itself. Pyramids and castles, rocks and reefs, icebergs and ships, towers and domes; everything belonging to the grand and magnificent could be seen in this distant harbour; the half obscured sun shedding his mellow light upon it, gave it a rich and dazzling lustre. They were really 'castles in the air', formed of the clouds. Casting my eyes upwards, I was astonished in beholding another cloud stratum, far above the lower one; it was what is commonly termed a 'mackerel sky', the sun shining faintly through it. The balloon seemed to be stationary; the clouds above and below appeared to be quiescent; the air castles in the distance stood to their places; silence reigned supreme; it was solemnly sublime; solitary and alone in a mansion of the skies, my very soul swelled with emotion; I had no companion to pour out my feelings to. Great God! what a

184

scene of grandeur! . . . The solemn grandeur—the very still-
ness that surrounded me seemed to make a sound of praise.

G. W. WISE

PLAYTIME IN THE SKY

I

IN A BALLOON

I am in a very small balloon over Surrey on the last day of a
beautiful May.

So light is the wind that on that little voyage three hours and
a half were taken to travel sixteen miles, from Roehampton
to Betchworth. There is scarcely a cloud in the sky. The sun is
hot, and the balloon being one of gold beater's skin inflated
with hydrogen, is very lively. . . . The basket is quite tiny; two
men in it would be a crowd! The rigging and all the appoint-
ments are designed for lightness. I am alone and as the hours
pass the loneliness becomes rather oppressive. This is quite
different from aeroplaning, for there is little to occupy the
attention, and scarcely anything to do with the hands. Plenty of
time to look around and down!

Very slowly I approach a big wood. It would rather express
the situation were I to say that very slowly a big wood comes
nearer to the balloon, for there is no sense of movement, and
the earth below seems to be moving slowly past a stationary
balloon. As the wood comes nearer I watch the aneroid and get
a bag of ballast ready. For I know that over the wood the air
will be slightly cooler, with probably a slight down-draught due
to convection, and that the balloon will immediately begin to
descend; and I shall have to check that descent by throwing a
little ballast.

Fifteen hundred feet up and almost absolute silence, broken
occasionally by the barking of a dog heard very faintly, or by a
voice hailing the balloon, and by an occasional friendly creak of

the basket and rigging if I move ever so slightly. Then quite suddenly I am aware of something new.

The balloon has come down a little already, and I scatter a few handfuls of sand and await the certain result. But my attention is no longer on that, it is arrested by this new sound which I hear, surely the most wonderful and the sweetest sound heard by mortal ears. . . . It is the combined singing of thousands of birds, of half the kinds which make the English spring so lovely. I do not hear one above the others; all are blended together in a wonderful harmony without change of pitch or tone, yet never wearying the ear.

By very close attention I seem to be able at times to pick out an individual song. No doubt at all there are wrens, and chaffinches, and blackbirds and thrushes, hedge-sparrows, warblers, greenfinches, and bullfinches and a score of others, by the hundred; and their singing comes up to me from that ten-acre wood in one sweet volume of heavenly music.

There are people who like jazz!

C. C. Turner—*Old Flying Days*

II

IN AN AEROPLANE

One day we put a couple of miles between us and the earth. The sky is blue. Round about are isolated lumpy clouds, dazzling white on the sun-side, grey in shadow, peaks and domes above, crevasses and caverns below. Between them the dull-hued earth is visible, its fields and towns a mere make-believe of a nursery in Lilliput. Forget for a moment that long irregular broad-scarred line where the earth's fair skin is ravaged as by some foul disease. Forget the points of red flame that gleam without ceasing, now here, now there, along that hideous line, here singly, there in ordered rows. Forget the dark smoke that rolls up from some burning town miles away.

Ahead of us is a huge dome-like mass which might be a hundred S. Paul's Cathedrals rolled into one. It is irresistible, but at the last moment we refrain, the lever is pulled back, and our chariot climbs over that dome of dazzling vapour that looks like snow as if the wheels were veritably ploughing its surface. Over its top we go, and down the other side, the pilot keeping up the illusion of 'taxy-ing' over the snow. Then, instead of leaving it we return sharp to the left, with the right wing canted up, and make a complete circle of the dome, the left wing sometimes brushing it and it almost seems, in danger of being damaged.

Up here we are part of the wind itself, and we are slowly nearing home, for the wind is from the east. Whether we charge a cloud from front, or rear, or flank, our motion is relatively to it the same. We come to a series of little clouds with white peaky tops. We fly through the peaks and I look back almost expecting to see the tops of them go falling down like thistles beheaded by a swinging cane. We roar through a big grey monster, and instantly are immersed in dense fog. Then out again into the bright sunshine; and, looking back, no sign of our passing save a swirl of the vapour, which quickly subsides.

C. C. Turner—*Old Flying Days*

FIRST FLIGHT

Dedicated to the R.A.F. by the Author, June 1941

The pilot took his seat. Life like a wind
Came rushing out of nowhere and laid hold
Of this day's creature. All three two-spoked wheels
Became three wheels of many spokes and sang,
And, singing, vanished utterly and left
Serene blue sky where they had been, and song.
The airplane trembled, stirred, and bumped along,

187

The wind became a hurricane, the ground
Leaped back a blur, the creature took the air.

And now it leaned up sharply; the wide world
Tipped sharply down, and ran off on both sides.
The wings spread to the sun an hour high,
Red as a window of the Apocalypse,
The taut wings headed west, the earth spun east.

The airplane levelled out, its triple heart
Beat like a law of cosmos in the brain.
High and aloof, it lost the sense of speed,
It stood serene and let the earth go past
Beneath it on its natural, eastward way.
The movement of the land was grave and slow;
Towns, forests, and the river winding on,
The patchwork of square fields in brown and green,
Slid under in a rhythmic dignity.

The flier, new to flight, had looked for speed,
This quiet was the quiet of a psalm.
The great clouds stood unhurried on each hand,
The land was calm and golden in the sun
As in the landscapes painted years ago.
The flier had not felt so still as this
Since he had sat with evening as a boy
Beside a trout stream, with a muted breath..
Serenity lay under on the world,
Peace lay below this creature fed on fire.

Beneath the poised, still plane the land unrolled
Its pattern of small towns and woods and fields.
The houses did not hurry. They stood white
And independent on their rugs of green,
They pointed up like tents against the weather;
They closed in something precious and alone.

The towns, though, were but little islands,
The rest was ocean, and the waves of leaves.
Trees were still chief citizens of earth,
They hemmed the new and metalled highways in,
They laced the edges of the smallest fields.

The farms were lovelier than this flier dreamed,
Each a little universe entire.
They had their backs in sun and feet in water,
Their hearts were barns. The history of man
Was in the scrollwork of the paths he made
From house to well, from orchard to the brook.

From his high place the flier saw that things
That meant most to a man were very old:
A tree before a door, earth turned in furrows,
A pathway by a brook, an old mill dam,
The sound of bees and cowbells, clean, new grass,
An acre he had planted, sunlit panes,
A small piece of the world which he had made
To blossom and to breed his children on.
A man might fly above the hills or hide
Away from green, in cities of made stones,
The ancient loyalties still found him out,
They came on him through air and through blue steel,
They held him in their everlasting arms,
With all his new-found softness and strange toys,
The mother held him close and turned him round
As she turned on her way about the sun.

In a low deep light the flier saw
Four little horses and a man behind
Turning hair-like furrows far below,
And they were one and beautiful past words.
They went like evening, climbing up the world;
They moved, but all their motion was like peace.

And now the solemn eastward march of earth
Was bringing on the mountains into view,
The day lay on the western sides of them,
The night was heaped behind their eastern walls.
The sun was but a flake of molten fire
Upon the farthest range. The sun was gone.
Only great wings of light in backward flight
Came up behind the world as all grew dark.

The mountains merged, subsided, little lights
Twinkled into being here and there.
Houses were lit, and towns prepared for night.
The sunset wings were folded down and down.
Along straight lines, faint little fireflies
Crawled home with people in them bound for rest.

The plane tipped, and he glanced above; the stars
Were out in millions on bright millions there.
He had never been so close to them as now,
So bright before, this man had never seen them
Flame upon flame, and sun upon great sun,
Hung in the void of space, with laws between them,
Carrying the substance on which they fed.
Sun upon sun, without seen hands to feed them,
Lit for the aeons, and a symmetry
Which men, ages ago, had known as God.

Vast powers reaching downward from the stars
Held the earth and airplane in their hands.
The heartbeat of the engine died away
Into a heartbeat mightier than the sea;
All these were grown together in one form:
The vigour in the sleeping trees below,
The secret life sealed in primeval rocks,
The small lamp fed on lightning down below.

Dark arrows in the ether overhead,
Winged messengers between the distant suns,
Whispered their way, and bound all things in one.

The plane reached over gracefully and reached
Two sudden arms of light towards the ground,
Moved in a lovely circle, headed down.
The world came up, and burst into bright day.
Speed hurtled back to furious life. The plane
Rushed on and settled, felt the stubborn ground,
Trembled, slowed, and turned. Its wheels ran down,
Its heart-beat fluttered once. The world stood still.

ROBERT P. TRISTRAM COFFIN

CLOUD

The airman takes a very different view of clouds than the earthman. Sometimes clouds that are a mere annoyance to the earthman may be a deadly peril to the airman; and again, clouds which turn the eaves into spouting fountains and fill the streets with mud may merely amuse the airman. Here is a vast rosy-flushed giant some 8,000 feet high, 50,000 feet long, 20,000 feet wide, good-humoured, smiling. A moment and the angle of the light is changed, and he is a slate-grey frowning mass, terrible. But the airman was never deceived, the monster's shape as seen from the aeroplane was that of an anvil, an inverted wedge, its apex resting on the shadowed earth. That is a typical form of the thundercloud; and sometimes their tops are like fairy cities wrought in gleaming snow, and to these fairy cities, which may be a mile or more high, the airman betakes himself 'on iron wings that climb the wind' knowing that he can leave them at will.

C. C. TURNER—*Old Flying Days*

CYCLONE

From Agra, with its book of kings, we flew to Jodhpur; a terrific storm on the way nearly proving our undoing. We had risen high above the Agra plain and were some seventy miles on our way when in the far distance a mighty brown wall seemed to rise sheer out of the earth, a barrier that mounted higher and higher and became ever more black and menacing, as though it would say, 'Thou shalt not pass.' We pressed on to meet the challenge, rising still higher until the altimeter registered 12,000 feet; but we might as well have risen to the stratosphere in the effort to get clear of the enemy for the dark brown wall rose higher than we did, its vanguard was already in touch with us, whistling and howling around our tiny aircraft like a legion of devils.

It was getting black as night, nothing was visible but the rampart of dark brown dust, sweeping onward in an attack which was evidently going to be of a desperately determined nature. It was plain that before many minutes we should be fighting for our lives in the air.

A terrific gust struck the 'plane, which shivered as a boxer might from a savage upper-cut to the jaw. There was no time to be lost. We must either turn about and seek safety in flight, or crash through the storm and trust to luck.

McIntyre never hesitated; he knew that the sane thing to do was to turn and, flying before the storm, make for the landing-ground at Agra. No other course was open to us under the circumstances ; once there we might effect a safe descent and let the fury of the tempest pass on and beyond us. It was a wise decision; and so making a wide circuit to the left in the darkness we tried conclusions with the hurricane. Those who have only battled with a dust storm on the ground, should see one in the air when seated in a tiny Moth!

We swirled along, slap-dash we burst into the very thick of the pursuing storm; gusts of the typhoon seemed to leap over us like harlequins in a pantomime. We were going all out; such a skedaddle was never witnessed. On we went, gaining on our pursuers and getting into a clearer atmosphere, but always with the storm close behind us, its force mobilized and trying once for all if it could not, by a tremendous effort, drive us from the air, and sweep us off the face of creation. It very nearly succeeded; only the skill of the pilot saved us.

I peered over the side of the cockpit; it was clear enough to make out the Agra aerodrome, and then I found myself touching earth and the 'plane gliding towards a walled enclosure. It pulled up; Mac and I leapt out and by a tremendous effort pushed it into safety under lee of the protecting wall. Not a moment too soon; the storm was at our heels, it had now reached the wildest pitch of intensity and we felt as though both the 'plane and ourselves might be worsted if the struggle went on much longer.

It galvanized us into even greater activity; we carried huge stones as though they were so many apples, anchoring them to the machine with rope that the resourceful Mac produced from apparently nowhere. We held on to the wings, for by now the fury of the wind and dust had closed in upon us, we clung to the 'plane resisting all attempts to force it from our hands and deliver it over to this devil's guild.

Gradually the cyclone passed, the deafening notes that sounded to us like the voice of Gehenna gave way to the hissing and bubbling that marks the rearguard of such an encounter, until all became comparatively quiet and resumed its normal composure.

P. T. ETHERTON—*First over Everest*

CIRCLET

Twilight falls like rain, like tears,
　To wash the bitter dust away,
A small still crescent moon appears
　Above the wreckage of the day;
The first spring month is in her ark,
　So silver-burning she
Curtseys and vanishes when dark
　Clouds journey from the sea;
She came too soon, her frailty bears
　Of joy the penalty.

FREDEGOND SHOVE

THE JOY OF FLYING

When heavy on my tired mind
　The world, and worldly things, do weigh,
And some sweet solace I would find,
　Into the sky I love to stray,
And, all alone, to wander round
In lone seclusion from the ground.

Ah! Then what solitude is mine—
　From grovelling mankind aloof!
Their road is but a thin-drawn line:
　Their busy house a scarce-seen roof.
That little stain of red and brown
They boast about!—It is their town!

How small their petty quarrels seem!
　Poor, crawling multitudes below;
Which, like the ants, in feverish stream
　From place to place move to and fro!

194

Like ants they work: like ants they fight,
Assuming blindly they are right.

Soon their existence I forget,
   In joy that on these flashing wings
I cleave the skies—Oh! let them fret—
   Now know I why the skylark sings
Untrammelled in the boundless air—
For mine it is his bliss to share!

Now do I mount a billowy cloud,
   Now do I sail low o'er a hill,
And with a seagull's skill endowed
   Circle, and wheel, and drop at will—
Above the villages asleep,
Above the valleys, shadowed deep,

Above the water-meadows green
   Whose streams, which intermingled flow,
Like silver lattice-work are seen
   A-gleam upon the plain below—
Above the woods, whose naked trees
Move new-born buds upon the breeze.

And far away above the haze
   I see white mountain-summits rise,
Whose snow with sunlight is ablaze
   And shines against the distant skies.
Such thoughts these towering ranges bring
That I float on a-wondering!

So do I love to travel on
   Through lonely skies, myself alone;
For then the feverish threat is gone
   Which on this earth I oft have known.
Kind is the God who lets me fly
In sweet seclusion through the sky!

           PAUL BEWSHER—*Dawn Patrol*

LAUS DEO IN EXCELSIS

The sullen cloud that screens the world below
Changes before my eyes to purest snow,
And peerless napery for mile on mile
Lies laden in the joy of Heaven's smile.
And all the time the little aeroplane
Plays with its shadow on that wondrous plain.
      And as for me, I nod
To mine own image bidden to the feast,
And for that moment, I am not the least
      Of all the Sons of God.

F. MacNeece Foster

THE LURE OF FLYING

... Some there are who travel for the thirst of great horizons, and the fever called in Northern Europe the 'Wanderlust', others take ship, or car, that they may have for companions those many fair-faced wanderers, Change and Variety; but no man or woman will ever have seen one-tenth of the earth's surface, or experienced the true height and depth of wonder unless they have taken wings and flown.

Flying can be a real love affair that gets into and occupies the mind. It is a dramatic entertainment that stretches outwards and inwards at the same time. In a curious tingling way it combines the beginning and end of movement. There are aviators, who maintain, not only that the air is the region in which it is easiest to keep awake and watchful, but that flying makes them no longer afraid of time. Of the four elements composing the human environment, air has a fourth dimensional gift, transcending the cold fatality of human limits and time-tables or the noisy insistence of mechanical clocks, and holding out already in its hand for its devotees and followers the skeleton keys that will unlock the future.

Those who go up to the clouds in trips and take their travel across the sky, in the simplicity of a small aeroplane, can bear witness to much that is eternal and elemental. They can see the morning awaken and leap from the ground in a new day, they can hear the loud triumphant shout of gangster gales, feel the ghostly touch of cloud curtain and storm, and become acquainted with the fadeless duck's-egg blue of the sky, always most tender in colour when it has high mountains for a neighbour.

First Over Everest

THE BEAUTY OF FLYING

29 September 23

This last summer I had a number of aeroplane journeys about Europe. I had flights in several of the big omnibus aeroplanes that fly on the more or less regular European services, and also I flew as the single passenger in smaller open machines. There is a delight and wonder in the latter sort of flying altogether lost in the boxed-in aeroplane.

.   .   .

I have renewed and strengthened my sense of the sweetness and beauty of air-travel—in the small open machine.

As I hung in the crystalline air above the mountains of Slovakia, far above the wooded hills and deep green gorges, with the culminating masses of the Little Carpathians heaped up to the right of me and the line of the White Carpathians away to the left, and ahead of me, still and distant, the striped fields and villages of the plain of Bratislava; and as I turned about and looked at the blue Moravian lands behind me, with every stream and pool picked out in molten silver by the afternoon sun, I was as near the summit of felicity as I have been in all my very pleasant life. Ever and again we overtook some little puff of cloud. There were little troops of bright white cloudlets that raced with us eastward, swift and noiseless; their shadows raced our own little shadow up the slopes and across the forest crests below, and their whiteness and their transitory cool embrace as we passed through them, enhanced by contrast the sunlit clearness and brightness of the outspread world.

For the first part of my flight that day I was accompanied by three other Czech machines. They were fighting aeroplanes. They came up abreast of me in the liquid air, and their aviators signalled to me, and then, suddenly, they dived and swept over in a loop and fell down like dead leaves for a thousand feet or so and righted themselves and flew home to Prague. I have seen such manœuvres before from the ground, but they are far more graceful and lovely when one floats above them and watches the aeroplane drop down like a falling kite, almost, it seems, to the spires and tree tops.

At last we began to descend, and circled down to Nitra, a place I had never heard of before, a wonderfully beautiful and, I should think, a very prosperous town, with a great church and many spires, and from the aerodrome at Nitra I started again two days later to return to Prague. The weather was unsettled, and the most hopeful time for flying was the early morning. I left Topolcany, where I had been staying, at dawn, therefore with a full moon shining brightly in a rain-washed sky, and after a little misadventure and a cut head in a ditch, for automobiles are much less safe than aeroplanes, and the roads that morning were wet mire, reached Nitra at sunrise and rose with the red blaze of the sun above the hills.

Sun and aeroplane seemed to soar up together. Never before had I been up in the air so early in the morning. All the little trees below were blobs and dots, but they cast shadows hundreds of feet long, and in the deep blue nooks and crannies of the gold-lit hills the white mists huddled.

The wind rose against us as we returned and blew a gale. We took four hours to make a journey that the other way, before the wind, had taken little more than two. Between Brunn and

Prague the aeroplane swayed and danced like a kite on its string and ever again found an air pocket and dropped a few score feet. But though I am but a moderate sailor, I do not get air-sick; and to sit loose and lax and unafraid, strapped into an open aeroplane, drenched in sweet air, is altogether different from being enclosed in an air omnibus. I had rather be four hours in an open aeroplane in a high wind than two in an automobile on a bad road or one in a Channel steamboat on a rough day.

Those two flights in Slovakia are among the very happiest experiences I have ever had in my life.

H. G. WELLS—*A Year of Prophesying*

ON THE WINGS OF THE MORNING

A sudden roar, a mighty rushing sound,
   a jolt or two, a smoothly sliding rise,
a jumbled blur of disappearing ground,
     and then all sense of motion slowly dies.
       Quiet and calm, the earth slips past below,
       as underneath a bridge still waters flow.

My turning wing inclines towards the ground;
   the ground itself glides up with graceful swing
and at the plane's far tip twirls slowly round,
     then drops from sight again beneath the wing
       to slip away serenely as before,
       a cubist-patterned carpet on the floor.

Hills gently sink and valleys gently fill.
   The flattened fields grow ludicrously small;
slowly they pass beneath and slower still
     until they hardly seem to move at all.
       Then suddenly they disappear from sight,
       hidden by fleeting wisps of faded white.

The wing-tips, faint and dripping, dimly show,
  blurred by the wreaths or mist that intervene.
Weird, half-seen shadows flicker to and fro
  across the pallid fog-bank's blinding screen.
    At last the choking mists release their hold,
    and all the world is silver, blue and gold.

The air is clear, more clear than sparkling wine;
  compared with this, wine is a turgid brew.
The far horizon makes a clean-cut line
  between the silver and the depthless blue.
    Out of the snow-white level reared on high
    glittering hills surge up to meet the sky.

Outside the wind-screen's shelter gales may race:
  but in the seat a cool and gentle breeze
blows steadily upon my grateful face
  as I sit motionless and at my ease,
    contented just to loiter in the sun
    and gaze around me till the day is done.

And so I sit, half-sleeping, half-awake,
  dreaming a happy dream of golden days,
until at last, with a reluctant shake,
  I rouse myself, and with a lingering gaze
    at all the splendour of the shining plain
    make ready to come down to earth again.

The engine stops: a pleasant silence reigns—
  silence, not broken, but intensified
by the soft, sleepy wires' insistent strains,
  that rise and fall, as with a sweeping glide
    I slither down the well-oiled sides of space
    towards a lower, less enchanted place.

The clouds draw nearer, changing as they come.
Now, like a flash, fog grips me by the throat.

Down goes the nose: at once the wires' low hum
　begins to rise in volume and in note,
　　till as I hurtle from the choking cloud
　　it swells into a scream, high-pitched and loud.

The scattered hues and shades of green and brown
　fashion themselves into the land I know,
turning and twisting, as I spiral down
　towards the landing ground; till, skimming low,
　　I glide with slackening speed across the ground,
　　and come to rest with lightly grating sound.

JEFFERY DAY

AN AMERICAN FLIES OVER ENGLAND

I still remember this flight across great little England, as something that pulls the heart-strings, I hardly know why. We flew for two hours and ten minutes from Croydon to Brough, near Hull, and during that time we had seen something of the country—or *felt* something of it—which the tourist afoot can but gradually realise. This indeed, is the wonder of flying: in a couple of hours you may achieve a feeling—realisation of what Shakespeare meant by his stately lines to 'This England'. Wizard as he was, it probably took William half a lifetime to figure it out: but up in the air one saw at once that England was just what he said—a *'jewel set in a silver sea'*.[1]

E. H. NELSON—*The First World Flight*

[1] '*This precious stone set in the silver sea,*
　Which serves it in the office of a wall,
　Or as a moat defensive to a house,
　Against the envy of less happier lands,
　This blessed plot, this earth, this realm, this England.'

King Richard II, II, I.

LONDON TO PARIS BY AIR

The droning roar is quickened, and we lift
On steady wing, like upward sweep of air,
Into the fleece-strewn heaven. The great plane
Draws to herself the leagues: onward we bear
In one resistless eddy towards the south
Over the English fields, trim-hedged and square,
And countless, winding lanes, a vast expanse
Of flattened green: huge shapes of shadow float
Inconsequent as bubbles: haunts of men
Stripped of their cherished privacy we note
And crawling multitudes within a town—
On all we rangers of the wind look down.

The coast-line swings to us: beneath our feet
The grey-green carpet of the sliding sea
Stretches afar, on it small, busy ships
Whose comet-tails in foamy whiteness flee:
We lift, and snowy cloudlets roam below,
Frail, wistful spirits of pure charity
Blessing the waters: like green marble veined,
The waves roll in upon the yellowing sand,
Then break to myriad, filmy curves of lace
Where they eternally caress the land:
Now low lies France—the kingdom of the breeze
Parts not the nations like the severing seas.

Down the wide river, jauntily outspread,
A fishing fleet comes seaward, to our eyes
Mere walnut shells with autumn leaves for sails:
And now a fellow pilgrim of the skies,
Like a big insect droning past our flank,
Cruises to England home: before us lies

The rolling plain with its great, hedgeless strips
Of close-tilled fields, red roofs, and pointed trees,
The feathered arrows of the long French roads,
And all the stretch of quiet harmonies:
Then haven shows, and downward to earth's breast,
Like homing bird, we wheel and sink to rest.

LORD GORELL

STARSCAPES—THE GRAND CANYON

We left Los Angeles at nine. A metal door clicked to; the plane took off. From my back seat on the left of the cabin I could see an aluminium wing, a small red electric lamp and the letters T.W.A., denoting the Lindbergh Line. And once more that feeling of 'dehumanization' and utter loneliness, that curious impression that no worlds exist inhabited by man, came over me. All trace of humanity was vanishing from the earth. People were the first to go; then animals, then cars. Of the poor old world that cannot do without us nothing remained but roofs and houses emptied of life, it seemed, by some mysterious cataclysm. Nothing but straight lines, triangles, squares and rhombs; a world of bleak geometry, of patterned fields and crazy pavements—the work of man; of veins and arteries, volutes, curves and corrugations, shirrs and spirals, dents and dimples—the work of wind and rain.

And now we were gazing down upon a wilderness chequered by interminable white roads that linked together little groups of houses. In the distance shimmered a lake of sun-bleached dust. From the height at which we were flying, a passenger who could not read the landmarks might fancy he was looking down on a derelict world, one of the strange and terrifying landscapes we see in photographs of Mars, the Moon and Saturn. On the bleak expanse each patch of vegetation showed like a strip of velvet or a sleeping monster's fire.

But who can hope to understand the infinite diversity of colour in relief that figures on the palette of our earth? One thing, at least, is sure: that seeming chaos of disorder is composed of zones of order, and not a feature of the landscape, not a colour but is due to some slow, insistent process of nature's chemistry. The least wrinkle on the desert's face, each ripple of the plain, is the work of an intelligence, the outcome of a will. How can we not marvel at the way that life, so fragile yet so obdurate, has made itself at home in every corner of the globe? ...

Without this bird's-eye view of the epidermis of the earth, our adventure would have lacked completeness. Another thing that struck us was the way in which each strand of the fabric kept separate and distinct. If a film in accelerated motion (like the films illustrating the growth of plants) were taken of the surface of the earth, we should see the countless strands of which it is made up rippling, ravelling, unravelling, clustering in knots and tresses, but always coming clear again. We should see the mountain-chains as solidified rivers interlocking and crossing each other at various angles—but never merging or losing their identity.

The plane was flying over a desert scored with geometrical figures of prodigious complexity, and hunched on it were mountain-masses shaped like the Sphinx and, like her, posted lonely and aloof on beds of stratified rock.

Passepartout summed up his views on flying in three words, 'Man has guts!' He was right. It seemed miraculous that two thin blades churning the clouds and two frail wings poised in delicate equilibrium could uphold in air the cabin with its fourteen berths and passengers, not to mention the pilots and crew.

Little by little our left wing unmasked the huge up-ended oyster of the Grand Canyon, the lock between Colorado River and Boulder Lake, blue as the water in a blue-tiled bathing-pool. Here and there what looked like milk-white water spouts seemed puncturing the smooth expanse of azure—though, at a near view, the surface would doubtless look unruffled. When we flew over them the airplane lurched. These air-pockets are the pot-holes on the King's Highway, the ancient royal road travelled by Henri III and Richelieu. For aviation is still in the stage-coach epoch with its jolts and travel-sickness and make-shift domesticities.

As one of our poets 'took the heather of the meadows for a trackless forest', I saw the dense forests below us as close-cropped pastures, fields of gorse and heather. On either hand lay the circles of Dante's *Inferno*, guarded by red Sphinxes, rising in majestic tiers. Far down in an abyss where stone dragons writhed and floundered, flowed the Styx. But Dante and Virgil would have been hard put to it to find a foothold on these dizzy cliffs.

JEAN COCTEAU—*Round the World Again in Eighty days*

VIII
Night Flight

POEM XXIII

Where are the cloud-fleets of day?
    Through the flooding dark
Works a lone 'plane on its way—
    A pure, steady spark.

Lost are the sails of the sun
    In their own night's sea;
Still the gleam ends not, toils on—
    Flies blind—patiently.

           ELIZABETH DARYUSH—*The Last Man*

NIGHT FLIGHT

The Grand Nassau Balloon, 1836

Nothing in fact could exceed the density of night which prevailed during this particular period of the voyage. Not a single object of terrestrial nature could anywhere be distinguished; an unfathomable abyss of 'darkness visible' seemed to encompass us on every side; and as we looked forward into its black obscurity in the direction in which we were proceeding, we could scarcely avoid the impression that we were cleaving our way thro' an interminable mass of black marble in which we were imbedded, and which, solid a few inches before us, seemed to soften as we approached, in order to admit us still farther within the precincts of its cold and dusky enclosure. Even the lights which at times we lowered from the car, instead of dispelling, only tended to augment the intensity of the surrounding darkness, and as they descended deeper into its frozen bosom, appeared absolutely to melt their way onward by means of the heat which they generated in their course.

As the intensity of the darkness yielded to our approach, we could obtain some faint idea of the nature of the country which lay beneath us. At these times we appeared to be traversing large tracts of country partially covered with snow, diversified with forests, and intersected occasionally with rivers, of which the Meuse in the earlier part of the night, and the Rhine towards the conclusion, constituted as we afterwards learned, the principal objects both of our admiration and of our conjectures. Nothing could be more interesting than the glimpses which these mysterious approximations would occasionally permit us to enjoy. Slowly descending, as it seemed to us, from a region where darkness formed the only subject of our contemplations, at first some faint hallucination, (but whether of earth or air we could but doubtfully determine), would appear invading the obscurity of the sable vault immediately beneath us, and giving us the first notification of our approach to something that owned a form and acknowledged the laws of the material world. Gradually as we drew nigh, these mysterious appearances would insensibly extend themselves in space, strengthening in their outlines, and becoming more definite in their form, with an effect, which to render it more intelligible, we can only compare to that produced while, looking through a telescope during the process of its adjustment, the confused and shadowy features of some distant prospect are made to pass slowly through every gradation of distinctness ere the proper focus be at length obtained.

T. MONCK MASON—*Aeronautica*

FLYING AT DUSK

There is no sun:
But in the West there glows
A sea of rose.
The day is done;
And slowly fades in robes of flaming light
Before the night.

Below me lies
A mist of deepest blue
Which stains the view
With sapphire dyes,
And all the countryside below is kissed
With dim blue mist.

Here in the sky,
I see the day is gone
And dusk creeps on;
And as I fly
I know that, for the first time, from the air,
The world looks fair.

Never before
Has beauty filled my eyes
From towering skies.
I never saw
Earth look romantic from the heights above,
But Dusk brings Love.

PAUL BEWSHER—*The Bombing of Bruges*

NIGHT FLIGHT

The more man can enlarge the frontiers of mystery, the better for his health of mind. Storm and lightning cater generously for our sense of wonder, and those who travel from one city to another by the Valkyrie's route find still subtler, yet more awe-inspiring Valhallas opening up to the imagination. This marvellous flight widened our experience of the natural world and, without breaking across its boundaries, extended them.

If sleep had prevented me from seeing the oil wells, it had made known to me immeasurably stranger regions and proposed still darker mysteries than did our flight through the darkness. Yet, even if it proved that we must look elsewhere for Wagner's aerial cavalcades and Goethe's Witches' Sabbaths, that night flight showed us sights as wonderful as any we encountered on our journey round the world.

I have no patience with certain 'highbrows' who shrug their shoulders at the Sphinx or the Acropolis. More likeable is the attitude of such as pay homage to those glories of the past—to whose gradual perfection so many pioneering spirits gave their best—and set out to praise their beauty from a new angle.

The pageantry of storm and cloud we saw that night was older than the hills, yet new to us because the insect in whose belly we were travelling flew through the thick of it. Just behind a cloud-bank, on our right, the sky was freaked with a silver trellis-work of lightnings. Beneath us, on our left, a cavalcade of clouds moved ponderously past, screening the world below. Peering down through rifts, we saw new stars added to the firmament, new gulfs of darkness added to the night. For Passepartout the head-lights of the unseen cars were 'comets flying backwards'.

Now and again the clouds closed in on us and we seemed to be flying through a welter of soap-suds that became transparent when the lightning flashed across them. The moon was rising and, at the rare moments when the lightning failed, the myriad foam-flakes seemed to condense into a solid green-glimmering mass through which, between the snowdrifts and icebergs of an arctic sea, the airplane was forcing its way north.

Sometimes our ear-drums seemed to split and let the sound of the propellers come roaring in, then once more it dwindled to a distant drone—when altitude had choked our ears again.

Some passengers were asleep, others reading. The stewardesses glided between the chairs, keeping watch on those who read and slept, blind to the splendour that celestial dynamos were shedding on the sky. Like pale, limpid tendrils flattened against the glass of an herbarium, ponds of light flickered incessantly on the panes, while great clouds billowed round us

in a mighty cavalcade like that which lured Tolstoi's Prince
Andrew from his dream of glory.

JEAN COCTEAU—*Round the World Again in Eighty days*

NIGHT RIDES WITH THE MAIL PLANE

I

Loud motors batter emotion to silence,
And Earth becomes a thing of movement
Receding in a swift and certain way
To a setting of flat black. Whirring blades
Of metal cut the blue, and a night wind
Slides down a grey wall of cloud,
And sweeps the dark carpet of the world below.
Now we begin the long climb into night,
Towards a jagged horizon where stars burn gold.
Shadows thick as wool blur paths of the air.
Arrow-wise the plane speeds, a sullen
Warning to night; it crosses a moon-white field.
Lapping tides of a sudden body of water
Mingle music with a world of curious things.

Now the plane, wing-soft, bends around
The moon's river, and stray clouds—heaven's trees—
Blow by in high hot air. Dew is on the hour.
The mountains are adrip with light,
And stare up at us like silken fawns.
Shadow waves are stretched across
Bending wheat fields, and Dawn comes
In a cream light, climbing through fog,
Like spires of white stars . . .
My soul's frail door swings wide—
The hard bright steel wings mount

A step or two from heaven,
And I am God's nearest neighbour.

2

Peace is spread velvet-like through a wind-blurr'd world;
The plane, supple as a fish, swims through sea-heavy air,
And dusk moves into the lane below. Wind
Plays with the tops of apple-trees. Slow sheep move
Into a barn, and two birds awake and sing and sleep again.
Now comes a dirge from deep trees whose hungry roots
Know feeding and death's tranquility. I hurl thoughts
At the hours that pass, while the plane lifts higher
With the way of wings, leaving the blue-eyed grass
Far behind, and pools that lie in knowing silence.
Flashing down a stream of cloud light,
It crosses a moon-crazed sea. But even
In these airs, your voice pursues me,
And I fear your loveliness more than sky.

Now the sun comes up from its sleep in flowers
That closed their petal doors on night.
Why do I love all things that are fragile?

3

The chug of tractors sounds faintly like bee's hum.
Now we rise and below us is a yellow sea of grain.
There come shadows on the faces of many meadows,
Like spotted tiger lilies. Puffy clouds
Are white turkish towels hung on a mountain rack.
Purple settles on a torchless night,
And rivers lie hidden against black sycamores.
Now there is a glint of sand,
And colours are woven into the pattern,
Crouching with morning light. . . .
There is a silver foil along the edge of a lake,

And the colour of dust. The plane flies on
With the will of steel, from the chill pursuit
Of high air. Cities lie far below like strange
Jewel-eyed snakes that spring into night's hungry mouth.

We coast lower through tier on tier of clouds
From the ever altering skies. Starlight wavers
Through the top branches of trees, where an oriel's
First call is lost in the pounding motors.

You, minding the stern purpose of your control stick,
Are silent. . . .

ISOBEL STONE

THE LIGHT AT BOLLING FIELD

I watch the monster fire-fly of the night
   Caught in a network of invisible strings,
Making the heavens about him dark and bright
   With the closing and unclosing of his wings,
And think what pilot on the moonless air,
   Stemming the cloudy gulfs where stars turn dim,
Is pulsing towards that intermittent flare
   With eyes astrain for sight of home and him.
How many a pharos of the infant world
   Thus welcomed wanderers from roaring seas
To harbours where the waves were scarcely curled,
   And some white temple where they bent their knees
And hung the gift they vowed in danger sore!
   Flash on, far beacon of the sky's green shore.

JUDGE STAFFORD

THE NIGHT MAIL

The black rain falls down in a steady pour;
The stormy heavens flash a blinding light,
Now bar the windows up, and shut the door;
Not even a bird would brave the world tonight.

Not even a bird?—Above the thunders' drum
I hear the sound of some one there who flies,
Someone who travels with a roaring hum-m-m,
In a high ship with yellow lights for eyes.

The wet wind sweeps him fiercely from his path;
Around him white-hot bolts of lightning play;
The thunder hurls at him its booming wrath—
And he goes calmly on his zig-zag way.

What is the cargo that he carried there?
How is it precious, that it cannot wait?
Oh! You who tempt the heavens, have a care!
But he goes forward like unchanging Fate.

Forward and upward! with a steady sail;
Battling his way across the furious skies—
Night after night he carries on the mail;
And none will know his name, unless he dies.

NAOMI C. KATZ

IX
Men and Machines

ABOVE THE CLOUDS: AN AIRMAN'S TE DEUM

Now Faith again has birth.
Of all the astral gifts, this is the pride,
A simple faith, alas, too oft denied
        Upon the sceptic earth.
For in the air, it follows that I must
Cast doubt aside, and gladly take on trust
Each bolt, strut, wire, the fabric or the wings,
And half a hundred unsubstantial things
        The which to doubt were Death;
        And so with every breath
And every wordless beauty of the sky,
My soul, for very joy, proclaims God nigh—
        With gathering force until
I feel, despite the vastness all around,
That not one sparrow falleth to the ground
        Without Almighty will.
        And all His words come true:
Eye hath not seen, nor tongue of man may speak
These glorious meads, which God Himself may seek
        To think on Love anew!

                                    F. MacNeece Foster

THE VICTORIES

O divine summits and O unascended solitudes!
O alone soaring over care and stain!
Who without wing shall set foot upon your pinnacles?
Or who your spaciousness of light attain?
Flames in the dawn-cold, towering incredible,
When else the earth is shadow-drowned and prone,
Veiled and unveiled by the misty-footed winds that guard
Bright chasm and black gulf round a thunder-throne,

Realmed with a vision beyond reaches of mortality,
Thither some splendour in the mind aspires,
Sharing the terror of your dark, tumultous sisterhood,
Silent in glory as of chanting quires.
Changing and changeless, O far-illumined Presences
In apparition from some world august,
Up from this flesh have you drawn us, as in ecstasy
That thirsts to elude this forfeiture of dust.
Even on your last heights man has set his perilous foot,
And mid the void as on some dazzling shore
Stands in the vast air, stricken and insatiate,
Wingless, a spirit craving wings to soar.

Now at last voyaging a fabulous dominion
Surpassing all the measures of his kind,
He, a free rider of the undulating silences,
Has in himself begotten a new mind;
Made him a companion of the winds of Heaven, travelling
Unpaven streets of cloudy golden snows,
Piercing forlorn mist, cold though it encompass him
Like a dead mind that nothing sees or knows,
Vacant, a cavern fleecy and immaterial,
A soundless vapour that he pulses through,
Suddenly emerging, and swims into the sun again
And steers his path up toward the topless blue;—
Towers in the frosty flame—apparelled mystery
Of brain-intoxicating sharp sapphire
Round him and above him, throbbing in the midst of it,
A daring, a defiance, a desire!

Mote in the hollow vast, drowned amid the vivid light,
Invading far and far the virgin sky,
Charioting with beats of fire, the fiery-beating heart of man
(O heart of flesh, O force of dread!) on high!
Careless of death is he, riding in the eagle's ways

Above the peak and storm, so dear a sting
Drives him unresting to strive beyond the boundaries
Of his condition, being so brief a thing,
Being a creature perishable and passionate,
To drink the bright wine, danger, and to woo
Life on the invisible edge of airy precipices,
A lover, else to his own faith untrue,
Giving the glory of youth for flower of sacrifice
Upon the untried way that he must tread,
So that he savour the breath of life to the uttermost,
Breath only sweet when all is hazarded.
Is it that, moving in a rapture of deliverance
From chains of time and paths of dust and stone,
Serving a spirit of swiftness irresistible,
He makes his pilgrimage, alone, alone,
Seeking a privacy of boundlessness, abandoning
A self surpassed, yet other worlds to dare?
Nay, in that element hailing his predestinate
World, and exulting to be native there?

LAURENCE BINYON—*The Sirens*

FLYING CHARACTERS
THE AGE OF THE GIANTS

It remained for the later years of the nineteenth century to produce men who were content to ascertain the nature of the support the air would afford before attempting to drive themselves through it.

Of the age in which these men lived and worked, giving their all in many cases to the science they loved, even to life itself, it may be said with truth that 'there were giants on the earth in those days', as far as aeronautics is in question. It was an age of giants who lived and dared and died, venturing into uncharted space, knowing nothing of its dangers, giving, as a man gives to his mistress, without stint and for the joy of giving. The science of today, compared with the glimmerings that were in that age of the giants, is a fixed and certain thing; for the great major problem vanished in solution when the Wright Brothers made their first ascent. In that age of the giants was evolved the flying man, the new type in human species which found full expression and came to full development in the days of the war, achieving feats of daring and endurance which leave the commonplace landsman staggered at thought of that of which his fellows prove themselves capable. He is a new type, this flying man, a being of self-forgetfulness; of such was Lilienthal, of such was Pilcher; of such in later days were Farman, Blériot, Hamel, Rolls, and their fellows; great names that will live for as long as man flies, adventurers equally with those of the spacious days of Elizabeth. To each of these came the call, and he worked and dared and passed, having, perhaps, advanced one little step in the long march that has led toward the perfecting of flight.

Considering the flying man as he appeared in the war period, there entered into his composition a new element—patriotism—which brought about a modification of the type, or, perhaps, made it appear that certain men belonged to the type who in reality were commonplace mortals, animated, under normal conditions, by normal motives, but driven by the stress of the time to take rank with the last expression of human energy, the flying type. However that may be, what may be termed the mathematising of aeronautics has rendered the type itself evanescent; your pilot of today knows his craft, once he is trained, much in the manner that a driver of a motor lorry knows his vehicle; design has been systematized, capabilities have been tabulated; camber, dihedral angle, aspect ratio, engine power, and plane surface, are business items of drawing office and machine shop; there is room for enterprise, for genius, and for skill; once and again there is room for daring, as in the first Atlantic flight. Yet that again was a thing of mathematical calculation and petrol storage, allied to a certain stark courage which may be found even in landsmen. For the ventures into the unknown, the limits of daring, the work for work's sake, with the almost certainty that the final reward was death, we must look back to the age of the giants, the age when flying was not a business, but romance.

E. C. VIVIAN—*A History of Aeronautics*

IN MEMORY OF A BRITISH AVIATOR

On those young brows that knew no fear
   We lay the Roman athlete's crown,
The laurel of the charioteer,
   The imperial garland of renown,
While those young eyes, beyond the sun,
See Drake, see Raleigh, smile 'Well done'.

Their desert seas that knew no shore
   Tonight with fleets like cities flare;
But, frailer even than theirs of yore,
   His keel a new-found deep would dare:
They watch, with thrice-experienced eyes
What fleets shall follow through the skies.

They would not scoff, though man should set
   To feebler wings a mightier task.
They know what wonders wait us yet.
   Not all things in an hour they ask;
But in each noble failure see
The inevitable victory.

A thousand years have borne us far
   From that dark isle the Saxon swayed,

And star whispers to trembling star
   While Space and Time shrink back afraid,—
'Ten thousand thousand years remain
For man to dare our deep again.'

Thou, too, shalt hear across that deep
   Our challenging fleets of thought draw nigh,
Round which the suns and systems sweep
   Like cloven foam from sky to sky,
Till Death himself at last restore
His captives to our eyes once more.

Feeble the wings, dauntless the soul!
   Take thou the conqueror's laurel crown;
Take—for thy chariot grazed the goal—
   The imperial garland of renown;
While those young eyes, beyond the sun,
See Drake, see Raleigh, smile 'Well done'.

ALFRED NOYES

THE PILOT

He is liege of wind and thunder,
And desperate resolute things.
   On the market-skies
   His spirit buys
A drink of death on desolate wings.
   His hands
   Hold Fate.
   He stands
   Like Hate
Between the winds and under
   The flashing brim
   Of the waters, slim
U boats wilt at the sight of him.

He rides the wild cloud-horses
On tracks of polar gold.
>His heart is hound
>Of the hunting-ground
Where the ghostly stags are foaled.
>Through hives
>Of stars,
>He drives
>His cars
Along moon-metalled courses.
>His feet are shod
>With lightning rod,
To walk the living hand of God.

F. V. BRANFORD—*Titans and Gods*

THE SCOUT-FIGHTER

He, the perfect pilot, knows
The life of every wind that blows
Along the aerial street.
He, High heaven's arch-athlete,
Trembles on the perilous keys
Of Death's unmortal ecstasies,
Weaving out of rushing fears
The stable rhythm of the spheres.

F. V. BRANFORD—*Titans and Gods*

THE GROUND STAFF

It is impossible to over-estimate the importance of the ground staff; reliability, safety, and economy—three foundation stones on which the goodwill of aviation must be erected—depend on their efficiency. It is true to say that the man on the ground keeps the machine in the air.

P. T. ETHERTON—*First Over Everest*

AIRMEN WHO DO NOT FLY

Because their work is not seen by the public it is not often realized that every time R.A.F. bombers return from the long, hazardous bombing raids over Germany, Italy, and enemy occupied territory the maintenance staffs have scored a success. These are the men whose task it is to keep the big bombers airworthy, and the result of their effort is obvious from the way in which aircraft of the Bomber Command are able to make almost nightly journeys, week after week and month after month, with mechanical failures so rare as to come as a shock to anyone in the Service.

Upon the standard of their work depends the safety not only of valuable machines but of crews of five or more. The maintenance staffs take such a pride in the condition of their particular bomber that there is keen competition in every squadron to have the best record of airworthiness for it. To each ground mechanic a bomber is 'my' aircraft. If it has done well on a raid he glows with pride. 'My aircraft did a good job over Berlin,' he will tell his colleagues and keen rivals in the mess that day. And the others will be pleased too—but just a tiny bit envious. When, as must happen sometimes in war, one of the raiders fails to return, its maintenance team feel a personal loss, not only for the crew, but for 'their' Whitley, Hampden, or Wellington.

Between ground staffs and the flying men there is a real and deep understanding, friendship and mutual respect. When the pilots, navigator, wireless operator, and gunners go out to their bomber as it stands on the airfield gently ticking over, ready for a raid, they know full well that that machine—every one of the hundreds of complicated parts of it—is in as perfect a condition as the maintenance men can get it. The ground men would regard it as base treachery to scamp a job on a long-range bomber (or any other machine for that matter), because they know that the normal hazards of a trip are bad enough without the additional worry of a faulty aircraft. It is just the same with the men who arm the guns and load the bombs into the racks. By long experience the flying crews have come to have unlimited confidence in them also. . . .

The maintenance crews work under the worst possible conditions. It is no secret that in war time aircraft cannot be kept in hangars because of the risk of attack. Instead, they are widely dispersed over the landing ground, and for that reason most of the maintenance work has to be done in the open, regardless of the weather. Snow, bitter winds, or heavy rain are not allowed to interfere. Every time a bomber has been on a raid it undergoes a thorough overhaul. The fitters, riggers, armourers, electricians, wireless mechanics, and instrument experts go over it with extreme care. Their trained ears and eyes can detect the slightest sign of danger or failure. The faintest hum in the engine is enough to tell them that something is wrong, and they are not satisfied until they have tracked it down. . . .

Whenever the squadron is about to go off on a raid they watch 'their' bomber start and they are there, waiting to see it come home. Immediately they start checking up on it. They dislike any change over to a new aircraft, and it is an advantage to keep them together as a crew, for they get to know one another's methods. The importance of the maintenance sections is recognized by every commanding officer in the Royal Air Force. One C.O. said recently that he liked to see every one of these men—fitters, riggers, armourers, electricians, wireless mechanics and instrument repairers, and so on—when they joined the squadron. He told each that he was just as important as anyone in the flying crews, and that upon him, equally with those who went on the raids, might depend the success or failure of an operation. Without the ground staffs, indeed, there would be no operations.

The Times, January 11th, 1941.

PILOT'S SUMMER

May 23rd

. . . On the dusty road back, gold with late sunshine, we saw the three Tutors up practising their inverted stuff for to-morrow's show for the public (Air Pageant, Hendon). After tea is the only time that the instructors get to do individual things, and for a week now they've been taking off at 5.30 to run through their piece. Up at 3,000 tonight to find smooth air and keep out of the bumps, trailing along three together in close formation upside down. It's incredibly hard to do decently. Roughly they spend fifteen minutes each trip on their backs. Curiously enough the standing on the head business doesn't worry them much. It's the weight of the legs and feet that trouble them, apparently it becomes harder and harder to keep your feet on the rudder bar. They tend to fall off all the time, and you get cramp in the muscles. Then there is that difficulty that even few people in the Service realize. The carburettor has to function upside down, so as they turn over they not only have to turn an oil cock to keep a small engine sump system going, but switch over the petrol, too, to feed another jet. And this jet gives them practically no throttle control. With only a very small adjustment they only have two speeds, full out and stop.

It's easily the cleverest show of the lot, and I tip my hat to them. And yet from the public's point of view it isn't frightfully spectacular. They can only goggle up and think, 'Well, there are three chaps upside down in good formation. That's very clever. Well, there they are, upside down.' And that's all there is to it.

And yet a ham-fisted son of a gun with only a handful of flying hours up his sleeve can thrill them to the core with damn fool tricks that are bad flying from the safety point of view and the easiest thing in the world. Take off at the crowd and hold her down until he's about fifty yards from them, with the needle off the clock. Then pull her up in a dirty great climbing turn and go up like a lift till he's hanging on his slots at a thousand or so feet. Engine roaring like a mad traction engine got loose in a tunnel.

Or else he can get a mile away and 3,000 up and then stick the nose down, slam the throttle through the gate, and not pull out until he's about twenty feet over their heads, wires and airscrew and everything screaming, exhaust making a racket like six express trains going through Crewe, and his airspeed needle going round on the third circuit, its spring wound up into a neat little ball. The crowd love it.

F. D. TREDRY—*Pilot's Summer*

MERMOZ

When the South American line was opened up Mermoz, ever the pioneer, was given the job of surveying the division between Buenos Aires and Santiago de Chile. He who had flung a bridge over the Sahara was now to do the same over the Andes. They had given him a plane whose absolute ceiling was sixteen thousand feet and had asked him to fly it over a mountain range that rose more than twenty thousand feet into the air. His job was to search for gaps in the Cordilleras. He who had studied the face of the sands was now to learn the contours of the peaks, those crags whose scarfs of snow flutter restlessly in the winds, whose surfaces are bleached white in the storms, whose blustering gusts sweep through the narrow walls of their rocky corridors and force the pilot to a sort of hand-to-hand combat. Mermoz enrolled in this war in complete ignorance of his adversary, with no notion at all of the chances of coming forth alive from battle with this enemy. His job was to 'try out' for the rest of us. And, 'trying out' one day, he found himself prisoner of the Andes.

Mermoz and his mechanic had been forced down at an altitude of twelve thousand feet on a table-land at whose edges the mountain dropped sheer on all sides. For two mortal days they hunted a way off this plateau. But they were trapped. Everywhere the same sheer drop. And so they played their last card.

Themselves still in it, they sent the plane rolling and bouncing down an incline over the rocky ground until it reached the precipice, went off into air, and dropped. In falling, the plane picked up enough speed to respond to the controls. Mermoz was able to tilt its nose in the direction of a peak, sweep over the peak, and, while the water spurted through all the pipes burst by the night-frost, the ship already disabled after only seven minutes of flight, he saw beneath him like a promised land the Chilean plain.

And the next day he was at it again.

When the Andes had been thoroughly explored and the technique of the crossings perfected, Mermoz turned over this section of the line to his friend Guillaumet and set out to explore the night. The lighting of our airports had not yet been worked out. Hovering in the pitch-black night, Mermoz would land by the faint glimmer of three petrol flares lined up at one end of the field. This trick, too, he taught us, and then, having tamed the night, he tried the ocean. He was the first, in 1931, to carry the mails in four days from Toulouse to Buenos Aires. On his way home he had engine trouble over a stormy sea in mid-Atlantic. A passing steamer picked him up with his mails and his crew.

Pioneering thus, Mermoz had cleared the desert, the mountains, the night, and the sea. He had been forced down more than once in desert, in mountain, in night, and in sea. And each time that he got safely home, it was but to start out again. Finally, after a dozen years of service, having taken off from Dakar bound for Natal, he radioed briefly that he was cutting off his rear right-hand engine. Then silence.

There was nothing particularly disturbing in this news. Nevertheless, when ten minutes had gone by without report there began for every radio station on the South American line, from Paris to Buenos Aires, a period of anxious vigil. It would be ridiculous to worry over someone ten minutes late in our day-to-day existence, but in the air-mail service ten minutes can be pregnant with meaning. At the heart of this dead slice of time an unknown event is locked up. Insignificant, it may be; a mishap, possibly: whatever it is, the event has taken place. Fate has pronounced a decision from which there is no appeal. An iron hand has guided a crew to a sea-landing that may have been safe and may have been disastrous. And long hours must go by before the decision of the gods is made known to those who wait.

We waited. We hoped. Like all men at some time in their lives we lived through that inordinate expectancy which like a fatal malady grows from minute to minute harder to bear. Even before the hour sounded, in our hearts many among us were already sitting up with the dead. All of us had the same vision before our eyes. It was a vision of a cockpit still inhabited by living men; but the pilot's hands were telling him very little now, and the world in which he groped and fumbled was a world he did not recognize. Behind him, in the glimmer of the cabin light, a shapeless uneasiness floated. The crew moved to and fro, discussed their plight, feigned sleep. A restless slumber it was, like the stirring of drowned men. The only element of sanity, of intelligibility, was the whirring of the three engines with its reassuring evidence that time still existed for them.

We were haunted for hours by this vision of a plane in distress. But the hands of the clock were going round and little by little it began to grow late. Slowly the truth was borne in upon us that our comrades would never return, that they were sleeping in that South Atlantic whose skies they had so often ploughed. Mermoz had done his job and slipped away to rest, like a gleaner who, having carefully bound his sheaf, lies down in the field to sleep.

Antoine de Saint-Exupéry—*Wind, Sand, and Stars*

FLIGHT

Climbing the levels of air they come,
   Swift as never an eagle flew,
Pioneers of the rolling cloud—
   The reaching wind—the abysmal blue.

Mountain and desert echo the drone
   Of the great grey birds that sing as they go;
Rivers mirror the tireless wings;
   Oceans throb and thunder below.

Does the news flash out to a host unseen—
   Columbus, Peary, all souls of fire
Whose courage ventured the unattained
   And won to the peak of a high desire?

Does the heart of Magellan quicken and beat,
   As it slumbers far from the coast of Spain,
Dream of a dim horizon line
   And the gleam of a virgin wave again?

Sky and sea shall remember them,
   And men in honour their names shall write
Who have woven around the spinning world
   The magic golden girdle of flight.

Ethel De B. Lasky

TO AN AVIATOR

Through the uncharted playground of the sky,
Where the four winds like laughing children run

And stars go singing, you have dared to ply
Your lovely craft, have kept tryst with the sun,
And plashed your wings adown those sapphire pools
Where merry tasks, suspended by a song,
Dance all the day, or a lost angel cools
His burning feet the limpid waves among;
There a white cloud of pinions brushed your face:
You have been partner with the age-old moon,
Have kept abreast of her in that swift race
When crowding stars, her sole spectators swoon.
And through the streets on tired feet we plod,
We earthbound mortals, envying you, a god.

E. Joyce Harrison

BYRD, EXPLORER

Born in a land of honey and light,
Bred with the hearth flame in his face,
Why did he dream in a tranquil night
   A dream of outer space?

What should a lad's gay fancy know
Of the wrath of winds when the storm rides free,
Of the bitter light on an Arctic floe,
   Or the surge of a midnight sea?

He cannot tell. But the dream is old
As his very heart;—from the deep of things
Sudden a flaw of alien cold,
   Sudden, a lift of wings. . . .

Something nameless and splendid—worth
The joy of youth and the peace of home:
A far hail, *Come to the end of the earth!*—
   An answering cry, *I come!*

N. B. Turner

UNSUNG

I watch him pass through the far-off sky,
Where, brittle and drained of light
The shell of an old moon hangs—and high
I catch the flash of his turning there,
A white spark winging along the air,
Then lost to sight.

Yet think you he travels the sky's blue road
Alone? From the world apart?
Up, out of the flying field, till glowed
That last high sparkle against the moon
There rides with him—be it night or noon
Some woman's heart!

And what achievement can man e'er write
In terms of those far-flung miles
Through lonely space, that can prove more might
Of faith and daring, than is her part,
Who, watching him bearing away her heart,
Yet waves—and smiles!

So honour the flashing ship that roars
Through the tenuous blue of day;
That hurls its shadow against the stars,
Or battles with death where the black sleet drives;
But honour as well the mothers and wives
Who wait and pray!

JULIE CLOSSON KENLY

FLIGHT

They are immortal, voyagers like these,
Bound for supreme and royal latitudes;
They soar beyond the eagle, where it broods,
With Venus and the evening Pleiades:

234

Far, in the blue pale Indies of the sky,
They plough, gold-prowed, the Arteries of Air,
Finding an unexplored dimension there—
They leave us Star Maps we may voyage by.

Not Galileo, with his dreaming power,
Nor great Columbus, master of the gale,
Chartered for Time, such harbours for man's flight.
Lured by another Odyssey, a Grail,
They climbed the heavens, Byrd in his white hour,
Lindbergh, an eagle sweeping through the night.

HAROLD VINAL

'OF FLYERS TOO I SPOKE'

Of flyers too I spoke, their resilient way
Over a course of continents, their homing
Through wind and fog, against error and expectation.
High spirits they had: gravity they flouted.
Often have your ambitions, flown too steep
For the power that engined them, lost grip and stalled:
In clouds you have lost your bearings; and in the desert,
Repairing a broken air-screw, envied the sand
That has no need to travel.
'Those were free agents: we are tied—' Listen,
Freedom is knowledge of necessity:
It is using the currents of air to waft your wings
And adverse ranges for test of climbing speed;
It is learning from drift how aim should be corrected,
And from emergency the extreme course;
Here flight is trimmed to meet capricious weather
And shaped by all elements shall master them.
It is also love revealed as the stern landlord,
And common calamity waking each house in a street
With a birthday present. It is the will to prove

Your case, though that last word
And clinching argument should be your death.
    Yes, you too, even now, the unregarded
Who were called hands (but those hands have been always
The ground mechanics of our wide-wing pride,
Made vision fast and cast molten imaginings)
—Into your hands history commits her spirit.

C. DAY LEWIS—A Time to Dance

THE AEROPLANE

Timid and bright as the crescent adventuring forth
From rainy eclipse,
Tentative yet as a bird Spring-released from the North
From the hangar she slips.

Pauses with hesitant grace, a shy dancing slave
Called by her lord,
Sky-drawn, advances resistless, a moon summoned wave,
A crusader's sword.

Over the aerodrome, taxis, somnambulist, swings
Her head to the light,
Suddenly rises, awake, with the sun on her wings
Stilly in flight.

Mounting, accelerates, leaps, an ethereal doe,
Her nose to the wind,
Silver-fleet, leaps through the cloud-hounds of thunder and
        snow,
Leaves them behind.

Slewing at last in blue air with an antelope grace,
The cloud-chase outrun,
Shying aslant on the hillside of infinite space,
She banks from the sun.

Will of the aeronaut, tautened life—tremulous wire
Lyre-strung to death,
Thrills through her framework the windy Daedalian fire,
The sun-passioned breath.

All her sleek fuselage, flaunting the speed-fluent curve
Peril inwrought
All her tense quickening of dauntless steel sinew and nerve
Answers his thought.

Sun-crowned he rests dream-fused with the joyous control,
Sky-set-apart
And the engine vibrates to the throb of man's aspirant soul
Beats with his heart.

Upward she climbs again—flattens on shadowy breast,
Dwindles—a swan
Rhyming the sun-track serene, in full flight for the West
She gleams and is gone.

MICHAEL SCOT

VOYAGE TO THE END OF NIGHT

A trance of force, the
Steel
Within a hurrying of wires
Spins.

The plane
Slices the landscape
High
In backward folds
Against the
     North

Beat the schedule! Oh
How speed

With vacuous purpose
Stuns

And darkens the argument
Of space

Close up, the sky
Is multiple and clangorous
With many trances
Like the trance of Steel

Who are these pilots
Wagering history
On the turn of one idea.

Whose crackling geometrics wake
Far birds of sorrow round
The tolling angels of the inland ways?

HAROLD ROSENBERG—*The Aeroplane Eye*

AN AERODROME

An aerodrome is a far finer sight than the bustle of a railway station. The sheds are full of mingled wings: great names, Imperial Airways, Air France, Luft-hansa, T.W.A., United, blazon their sides. The sounds of engines come down from the sky and echo among the buildings. The doors open for the big long-distance machines which travel to the corners of the earth.

H. MIGNET—*The Flying Flea*

X
Peril and Prayer

FROM 'ELEGY FOR THE FALLEN CLIMBERS'

The blackbird throws his shadow on the grass,
The sparrow on the rooftop, and the chouca
Turns where the climber cannot,
Circles above the glacier, and his wing
Touches the peak, not climbed this year.

Here, on the brittle edge of time, we stand,
There the airman waves in passing, and the chouca
Soars on the wind's resistance, turning, twisting,
Over the dazzling map, the world unfolded; and the shadow
Falls from the air.

Over clear ice and brittle stone, the shadow falls;
Over the turning and returning year,
Over the river and the factory and the bells,
Over the shouting and the silence, shadow
Falls from the world unknown.

There, in the equipoise of motion, bird and pilot,
Holding the substance and the shadow distant, rise
In the impossible element, expend their spirit,
Passioned by their own speed, till the spirit fails;
Substance and shadow meet.

There, where exhausted bird and pilot cannot land,
The shadow falls; there, from the lower peak,
The guides go down, the season ended;
Over the haunting shadow and the earth
Moves the indifferent air, the world not ours.

MICHAEL ROBERTS

WRECK OF THE UIVER

Out of the angry sky
Some dark Assassin hurled
A flaming assagai;
And the doomed airship fell
On to the desert sands,
A microcosmic Hell.

H. E. HOLLAND

AIR CRASH

What happened in those moments, those short few
Seconds, that seemed to each so timeless-long,
(Eternity had touched them) when they knew—
The modish, prosperous passengers, the strong
Young unreflective pilot, crew that here,
Fronting them, barring unescapably
Their road to life, was the all conqueror—
That they together faced what none could flee? . . .

Each one his own slow words, his acts delayed
(That were in truth so hurried) heard and saw,
Powerless—some other being its soul obeyed,
Some stranger published loudly his life-law . . .

Each had but one companion—knew, alone,
Himself, that till this hour he had not known.

ELIZABETH DARYUSH—*The Last Man*

A LITTLE PRAYER FOR THE MAN IN THE AIR

I never hear
The growling diapason of a plane
Up there,

The deep reverb'rant humming of a plane
Up there,
But up to God I wing a little prayer,
Begging His care
For him who braves the dangers of the air.

'God keep you, Bird-man, in your plane
Up there!
Your wings upbear, your heart sustain!
Give you good flight and oversight,
And bring you safe to earth again!'

I, too, have hostages with fortune up above,
And what may come to you may come to mine,
So, once again,—'God speed you as you rove!
Both you and mine to His care I consign.'

JOHN OXENHAM

IN MEMORIAM A. H.

Auberon Herbert. Captain Lord Lucas, R.F.C.

Killed 3rd Nov. 1916

.   .   .   .

That night I dreamt they sent for me and said
That you were missing, 'missing, missing—dead':
I cried when in the morning I awoke,
And all the world seemed shrouded in a cloak;
But when I saw the sun,
And knew another day had just begun,
I brushed the dream away and quite forgot
The nightmare's ugly blot.
So was the dream forgot. The dream came true.
Before the night I knew
That you had flown away into the air
Forever. Then I cheated my despair.

243

I said
That you were safe—or wounded—but not dead.
Alas! I knew
Which was the false and true.

And after days of watching, days of lead,
There came the certain news that you were dead
You had died fighting, fighting against odds,
Such as in war the gods
Aethereal dared when all the world was young;
Such fighting as blind Homer never sung,
Nor Hector nor Achilles never knew;
High in the empty blue.
High, high, above the clouds, against the setting sun
The fight was fought, and your great task was done.

Of all your brave adventures this the last
The bravest was and best;
Meet ending to a long embattled past,
This swift, triumphant, fatal quest,
Crowned with the wreath that never perisheth,
And diadem of honourable death;
Swift Death aflame with offering supreme
And mighty sacrifice,
More than all mortal dream;
A soaring death, and near to Heavens' gate;
Beneath the very walls of Paradise.
Surely with soul elate,
You heard the destined bullet as you flew,
And surely your prophetic spirit knew
That you had well deserved that shining fate.

Here is no waste,
No burning Might-have-been,
No bitter after-taste,

None to censure, none to screen,
Nothing awry, nor anything misspent;
Only content, content beyond content,
Which hath not any room for betterment.

God, Who had made you valiant, strong and swift,
And maimed you with a bullet long ago,
And cleft your riotous ardour with a rift,
And checked your youth's tumultuous overflow,
Gave back your youth to you,
And packed in moments rare and few
Achievements manifold
And happiness untold,
And bade you spring to Death as to a bride,
In manhood's ripeness, power and pride,
And on your sandals the strong wings of youth.
He let you leave a name
To shine on the entablatures of truth,
For ever:
To sound forever in answering halls of fame.

For you soared onwards to that world which rags
Of clouds, like tattered flags,
Concealed; you reached the walls of chrysolite,
The mansions white;
And losing all, you gained the civic crown
Of that eternal town,
Wherein you passed a rightful citizen
Of the bright commonwealth ablaze beyond our ken.

Surely you found companions meet for you
In that high place;
You met there face to face
Those you had never known, but whom you knew;
Knights of the Table Round,

And all the very brave, the very true,
With chivalry crowned;
The captains rare,
Courteous and brave beyond our human air;
Those who had loved and suffered overmuch,
Now free from the world's touch.
And with them were the friends of yesterday,
Who went before and pointed you the way;
And in that place of freshness, light and rest.

Where Lancelot and Tristram vigil keep
Over their Kings' long sleep,
Surely they made a place for you,
Their long-expected guest,
Among the chosen few,
And welcomed you, their brother and their friend,
To that companionship which hath no end.

MAURICE BARING

TO THE WINGLESS VICTORY

A PRAYER

Wingless Victory, whose shrine
By the Parthenon
Glorified our youth divine,
Hearken!—they are gone,
The young eagles of our nest,
They, the brightest, bravest, best,
They are flown!

Save thou the golden flight
That wakes the morn,
And dares the azure height,
The tempests scorn!

246

Save them o'er land and sea,
   In deeps of air!
Thy grace, where'er they be
   Ensphere them there!

Save them, the country's pride,
   Our wingèd youth!
And where they fall enskied,
   Save thou the truth,
   O Wingless Victory!

GEORGE EDWARD WOODBERRY

TO A CANADIAN AVIATOR WHO DIED FOR HIS COUNTRY IN FRANCE

Tossed like a falcon from the hunter's wrist,
A sweeping plunge, a sudden shattering noise,
And thou hast dared, with a long spiral twist,
The elastic stairway to the rising sun.
Peril below thee, and above, peril
Within thy car; but peril cannot daunt
Thy peerless heart; gathering wing and poise,
Thy plane transfigured, and thy motor-chant
Subduèd to a whisper—then a silence—
And thou art but a disembodied venture
In the void.

But Death, who has learned to fly,
Still matchless when his work is to be done,
Met thee between the armies and the sun;
Thy speck of shadow faltered in the sky;
Then thy dead engine and thy broken wings
Drooped through the arc and passed in fire,
A wreath of smoke—a breathless exhalation.
But ere that came a vision sealed thine eyes,

Lulling thy senses with oblivion;
And from its sliding station in the skies
Thy dauntless soul upward in circles soared
To the sublime and purest radiance whence it sprang.

In all their eyries eagles shall mourn thy fate,
And leaving on the lonely crags and scaurs
Their unprotected young, shall congregate
High in the tenuous heaven and anger the sun
With screams, and with a wild audacity
Dare all the battle danger of thy flight;
Till weary with combat one shall desert the fight,
Fall like a bolt of thunder and check his fall
On the high ledge, smoky with mist and cloud,
Where his neglected eaglets shriek aloud,
And drawing the film across his sovereign sight
Shall dream of thy swift soul immortal
Mounting in circles, faithful beyond death.

DUNCAN CAMPBELL SCOTT

COURAGE

Courage is the price that life exacts for granting peace.
The soul that knows it not, knows no release
From little things;
Knows not the livid loneliness of fear
Nor mountain heights, where bitter joy can hear
The sound of wings.
How can life grant us boon of living, compensate
For dull gray ugliness and pregnant hate
Unless we dare
The soul's dominion? Each time we make a choice, we pay
With courage to behold a resistless day
And count it fair.

AMELIA EARHART

248

HENRI POL: BIRD-LOVER

Died 15 June 1918

Bon soir, bon soir, Monsieur Pol!
For they tell me now you are dead.
Go, then; and peace to your soul,
And warm like a nest be your bed,—
A warm, well-feathered, well-weathered nest,
To give rest to the bird-wise head!

In the place of the Tuileries
It is eleven by the clock,
And the birds wait in the trees,—
They wait; but you do not come.
The small beaks sharpen and knock
On the boughs, and the quick throats trill,
And the bad little voices scold
Their lover because he is late
With the crumbs which he used to spill
In the pathway where other passed,—
Because, in service grown old,
He has failed them at last!
Hark, how they chatter and fret
And complain!—mate clamours to mate,
Crying aloud for the crumbs
Which you gave, which they ate:
Day goes, another day comes;—
Another: when will they forget?

A week, may it be, or a moon,
Or will it run on to a year,
Till the world is again in tune,
And the gardens all full of song—
Babblers begging a boon?

Will the legend of you last so long,
Will the tale be told to their young,
When you no longer appear?

Sweetly a story is told
How birds as they cross the brine,
Bound for the far-off land,—
Veering away to the west
Out of the southward line—
Come to a watery shoal
Sunk in a sea of glass:
No place for a foot to stand.
They poise, they hover and quest
This way and that; but in vain!—
There can they find no rest,—
There having come, they pass.

But because in the days of old
Just there a rock rose dry
For hungry claws to take hold
And tired wings ceased to fly,—
There, again and again,
They come; and the years pass by.

So, to the Tuileries,
Shall not the birds still come
When morning clocks strike eleven,
To sit and wait in the trees
For the legendary crumb,
And listen while old birds tell
Their tale which the tolling bell
Ever brings back to mind:
How to the ways of earth,—
Wingless, grey-haired, and kind
To them in their feathered mirth,

Came daily with hands outspread
A gentle Angel from Heaven,
Who was known in the breaking of bread?

And you, Monsieur Pol,—you too,—
Have you a ghost that can walk?
Have you an ear that can hear
Your songsters who prattle and talk
Of you—still of you—still of you?
Is there no room in the grave
For the seeing mind to remember
How boldly they used to behave
In spring, but how in December,
Cowed by the winter's cold,
When the sap of life ran dry,
When the little bodies were old,
And the wings too weak to fly,
They would come at your feet to lie,
So sure you would understand:—
'See me, see how I die!
O friend, reach me a hand!'
And you would gather and fold,
And gently bear them away
From the bitter perishing cold
And blast of the winter's day,
To a corner remote and calm
By the side of your own fire;
And there in a hollowed palm—
With charity filled like balm—
Give them their hearts' desire.

O gentle lover of birds,
Out of your place of rest
Throw to the world a crumb
Of the love that was in your breast,—

The love you bore for the dumb,
The compassion you had for the weak,
The broken, the frail, the meek,
When daily you used to come!

Man has learned how to fly!
His gods have given him wings,
And between them a heart of hate,
With a roaring fire for breath
To obey the bidding of kings:
And out of a storm-rent sky,
And over a stricken earth,
He leavens the land with dearth;
Wherever he goes he stings,
And his droppings are bolts of death!

Unto his hand hath come
The fruit of a thousand sowings;
This is the feast he makes
Out of the grain he hath strown;
So now he beholds the sum
Of all his comings and goings;
Now in the bread he breaks
His kingdom on earth is known

But when the Judgment comes,
And the Trumpet of Life is blown,
Surely you will arise
And stand among saints without shame.
Then shall the rabble and rout
Of the dead,—the slayer, the slain—
Watch you, patient and meek,
Gentle, tender, and wise,
Empty your pocket of crumbs,
Scattering food to your own,

Filling the hungry beak,
Calling your birds by name,
Choosing, and leading them out;—
There, with the banquet spread,
Unto your lovers made known
Once more in the breaking of bread.

LAURENCE HOUSMAN—*The Heart of Peace.*

XI
War

THIS IS THE HOUR

This is the hour when Courage knows her own,
   When hearts grow stern that else were gay and warm
When men and women are themselves the stone
   That holds these islands scatheless in the storm.

This is the hour when Freedom calls the names
   Of those that loved her when to love were well,
And each one answers as the rocks ran flames,
   As each would answer from the mouth of Hell.

This is the hour when Pleasure is no more,
   Ease of the lovely field, the tree, the flower;
Only the rocks, the long and valorous shore,
   The one unshaken heart. This is the hour.

Punch

A GOODLY HERITAGE

In the palace of our Lord
Wise and lovely things lay stored,
Deeply hidden, fenced about:
God made man to search them out.
There, held safe from age to age,
Slept the goodly heritage.

Soul was given him for a key
To unlock the mystery;
Heart for courage, eyes for sight,
Hands to handle it aright:
Through the fastened gates the prize
Gleamed like peeps of Paradise.

There, to bless his future need,
Man beheld new forms of speed,

Wondrous shapes in stone and steel,
Cube, and curb, and banded wheel,—
Steeds with fiery breath that run
Clad in traces of the sun:

Saw thick darkness change to light,
Feet up-mount equipped for flight,
Heaviest mass a lifted load,
And the world an open road,
Linking up from end to end
Man with fellow-man his friend.

In that vision blest his eyes
Watched the coming Paradise,—
City walls, whose upward span,
Statured to the scale of man,
Sheltered, amid streets of gold,
Fruits and fountains manifold.

So, for that far-distant day,
Sleep and sloth he put away;
For the gain of that great spoil
Body and brain gave up to toil;
In the palace of his Lord
Searched, and traced, and found reward.

Delving amid reefs and rocks,
He unloosed the magic locks;—
Wealth in mine and mountain stored,
Powers from deep waters poured,
One by one, with eager brain,
These he picked and made his gain.

Thus, with toil from age to age
Man brought home his heritage;
Wheresoe'er his shafts he drave,
Under wood, or wind, or wave,

Thence with ministry of might
Sprang new forms of life and light.

And of what his toil set free,
Now he holds the mastery:
Now to heart and hand and eyes
Come possession of the prize;
Now, as Time unbinds the spell,
Opens—lo, the pit of Hell!

. . . .

Through the sundered gates, behold,
   Statured to the scale of man,
Shattered streets more red than gold,
   Blood where once sweet waters ran!

Under cannon-guarded walls,
   Maimed and bruised with bleeding breast,
Sisyphus his burden hauls
   Up to heights that win no rest!

Scorched with fire, and scourged with steel,
   Blindly into darkness hurled,
Mad Ixion spins his wheel
   Round a desolated world.

Here the Tree of Life gives out
   Sickness from a leprous root;
Tantalus his lips of drought
   Strains toward a poisoned fruit.

Shrinks the fountain from its springs,
   Vintage all lies dead and done;
Icarus has filched the wings,
   Phaeton drives the sun!

      LAURENCE HOUSMAN—*The Heart of Peace.*

EYES IN THE AIR

Our guns are a league behind us, our target a mile below,
And there's never a cloud to blind us from the haunts of our
     lurking foe—
Sunk pit whence his shrapnel tore us, support-trench crest-
     concealed,
As clear as the charts before us, his ramparts lie revealed.
His panicked watchers spy us, a droning threat in the void;
Their whistling shells outfly us—puff upon puff, deployed
Across the green beneath us, across the flanking gray,
In fume and fire to sheath us and baulk us of our prey.

        Below, beyond, above her,
          Their iron web is spun:
        Flicked but unsnared we hover,
          Edged planes against the sun:
        Eyes in the air above his lair,
          The hawks that guide the gun!

No word from earth may reach us, save, white against the
     ground,
The strips outspread to teach us whose ears are deaf to sound:
But down the winds that sear us, athwart our engine's shriek,
We send—and know they hear us, the ranging guns we speak.
Our visored eyeballs show us their answering pennant, broke
Eight thousand feet below us, a whorl of flame-stabbed
     smoke—
The burst that hangs to guide us, while numbed gloved fingers
     tap
From wireless key beside us the circles of the map.

        Line—target—short or over—
          Come, plain as clock hands run,
        Words from the birds that hover,
          Unblinded, tail to sun;

Words out of air to range them fair,
From hawks that guide the gun!

Your flying shells have failed you, your landward guns are
dumb:
Since earth hath naught availed you, these skies be open! Come,
Where, wild to meet and mate you, flame in their beaks for
breath,
Black doves! the white hawks wait you on the wind-tossed
boughs of death.
These boughs be cold without you; our hearts are hot for this,
Our wings shall beat about you, our scorching breath shall kiss ;
Till, fraught with that we gave you, fulfilled of our desire,
You bank—too late to save you from biting beaks of fire—
Turn sideways from your lover,
Shudder and swerve and run,
Tilt; stagger; and plunge over
Ablaze against the sun:
Doves dead in air, who clomb to dare
The hawks that guide the gun.

GILBERT FRANKAU—*The Guns*

BOMBERS

Through the vague morning, the heart preoccupied,
A deep-in-air buried grain of sound
Starts and grows, as yet unwarning—
The tremor of baited deep-sea line.

Swells the seed, and now tight sound-buds
Vibrate, upholding their paean flowers
To the sun. There are bees in sky-bells droning,
Flares of crimson at the heart unfold.

Children look up, and the elms spring-garlanded
Tossing their heads and marked for the axe.

Gallant or woebegone, alike unlucky—
Earth shakes beneath us: we imagine loss.

Black as vermin, crawling in echelon
Beneath the cloud-floor, the bombers come:
The heavy angels, carrying harm in
Their wombs that ache to be rid of death.

This is the seed that grows for ruin,
The iron embryo conceived in fear.
Soon or late its need must be answered
In fear delivered and screeching fire.

Choose between your child and this fatal embryo.
Shall your guilt bear arms, and the children you want
Be condemned to die by the powers you paid for
And haunt the houses you never built?

C. DAY LEWIS—*Overture to Death*

NEWSREEL

Enter the dream-house, brothers and sisters, leaving
Your debts asleep, your history at the door:
This is the home for heroes, and this loving
Darkness a fur you can afford.

Fish in their tank electrically heated
Nose without envy the glass wall: for them
Clerk, spy, nurse, killer, prince, the great and the defeated
Move in a mute day-dream.

Bathed in this common source, you gape incurious
At what your active hours have willed—
Sleep-walking on that silver wall, the furious
Sick shapes and pregnant fancies of your world.

There is the mayor opening the oyster season:
A society wedding: the autumn hats look swell:

An old crocks' race, and a politician
In fishing waders to prove that all is well.

Oh, look at the war-planes! Screaming hysteric treble
In the long power-dive, like gannets they fall steep.
But what are they to trouble—
These silver shadows to trouble your watery, womb-deep
    sleep?

See the big guns, rising, groping, erected
To plant death in your world's soft womb.
Fire-bud, smoke-blossom, iron seed projected—
Are these exotics? They will grow nearer home:

Grow nearer home—and out of the dream-house
    stumbling
One night into a strangling air and the flung
Rags of children and thunder of stone niagaras tumbling,
You'll know you slept too long.

C. Day Lewis—Overture to Death

AEROPLANES

Iron birds floating in the sky
    Prey remorselessly
On the tiny, obscure dot
    That is some great city,
Below, men-insects rend and tear,
    Women wring hands of pity.

I have flown a hundred miles
    Over the blurred plain,
Dropping devastation and death,
    Blotting men's nerves with pain—
Their miserable cries were as tiny as insects'
    Calling their God in vain.

The sounds of their oaths and lamentations
    Could not even reach up to me,
The clouds were at peace, no tribulation
    Disturbed the sky-harmony,
Only my buzzing engine clanged
    And my heart beat dreadfully.

I laughed as I silently tossed blind Death
    Down on that insect people,
Dreadful it was in the peaceful sky
    To murder that insect people,
And never to hear a sound or cry
    Or a bell toll in a steeple.

I laughed when my last bloody bomb had gone,
    I shrieked high up in a cloud,
I wanted to fly in the face of their God
    And spit my disdain aloud,
I ripped through the terrified whistling air
    And burst through the earth's damp shroud.

Ah! it was blue there, wide and clear,
    Dancing alive in the sun,
And millions of bright, sweet cymbals rang
    Praising the deeds I had done,
And millions of angels cheering stood
    Deep-columned around the Sun.

And then I stood erect and cheered,
    Ay! shouted into the sky,
I filled the vast semicircle round
There was only the Sun and I,
The round, red, glittering, blazing Sun,
    And a fluttering human fly.

W. J. TURNER

THE SKY-SENT DEATH

'A German aeroplane flew over Greek territory dropping a
bomb which killed a shepherd, 1915.'

Sitting on a stone a Shepherd,
Stone and Shepherd sleeping,
Under the high blue Attic sky;
Along the green monotony
Grey sheep creeping, creeping.

Deep down on the hill and valley,
At the bottom of the sunshine,
Like great Ships in clearest water,
Water holding anchored Shadows,
Water without wave or ripple,
Sunshine deep and clear and heavy,
Sunshine like a booming bell
Made of purest golden metal,
White ships heavy in the sky
Sleep with anchored shadow.

Pipe a song in the still air
    And the song would be of crystal
Snapped in silence, or a bronze vase
    Smooth and graceful, curved and shining.

Tell an old tale or a history;
    It would seem a slow Procession
Full of gestures: limbs and torso
    White and rounded in the sunlight.

Sitting on a stone a Shepherd,
Stone and shepherd sleeping,
Like a fragment of old marble
Dug up from the hillside shadow.

In the sunshine deep and soundless
Came a faint metallic humming;
In the sunshine clear and heavy
Came a speck, a speck of shadow—
Shepherd, lift your head and listen,
Listen to that humming Shadow!

Sitting on a stone a Shepherd,
Stone and Shepherd sleeping
In a sleep dreamless as water,
Water in a white glass beaker,
Clear, pellucid, without shadow;
Underneath a sky-blue crystal
Sees his grey sheep creeping.

In the sunshine clear and heavy
Shadow-fled a dark hand downward:
In the shadow deep and soundless
Burnt a star-dropt thing of thunder—
Smoked the burnt blue air's torn veiling
Drooping softly round the hillside.

Boomed the silence in returning
To the crater in the hillside,
To the red earth fresh and bleeding,
To the mangled heap remaining:
Far away that humming Shadow
Vanished in the azure distance.

Sitting on a stone no Shepherd,
Stone and Shepherd sleeping,
But across the hill and valley
Grey sheep, creeping, creeping,
Standing carven on the sky-line,
Scattering in the open distance,
Free, in no man's keeping.

W. J. Turner

EDITORIAL IMPRESSIONS

He seemed so certain 'all was going well',
As he discussed the glorious time he'd had
While visiting the trenches.
      'One can tell
You've gathered big impressions!' grinned the lad
Who'd been severely wounded in the back
In some wiped-out impossible Attack.
'Impressions? Yes, most vivid! I am writing
A little book called *Europe on the Rack*,
Based on notes made while witnessing the fighting.
I hope I've caught the feeling of 'the Line',
And the amazing spirit of the troops,
By Jove, those flying chaps of ours are fine!
I watched one daring beggar looping loops,
Soaring and diving like some bird of prey.
And through it all I felt that splendour shine
Which makes us win.'
     The soldier sipped his wine,
'Ah, yes, but it's the Press that leads the way!'

  Siegfried Sassoon—*Counterattack and Other Poems*

THE ARMY OF THE PLANES

They are coming with the drumming of a million pinions
 humming
 And the purr of mighty motors that are all in time and tune.
Proudly soaring with the roaring of the thousand northers
 pouring
 Through the vast and hollow spaces sacred to the sun and
 moon.

They are racing into places filled with radiant star faces,
 Following the meteor's speedways and the comet's ancient
 lanes,

267

And the universe is shaking, and the waking earth is quaking
   At the terror and the marvel of the army of the planes.

Wings of wonder as they thunder sweep the rolling clouds
      asunder,
   Sailing great uncharted oceans of the empyrean blue;
Struts are singing, wires are ringing, swift propeller blades are
      flinging
   Spray of diamond dust and silver when they cut a star in
      two.

Hail the aerial squadrons forming, through the fields of azure
      storming,
   Battle birds the crimson war God to celestial combat trains,
Swooping down from viewless regions to the aid of earthly
      legions—
   Hail the glorious, victorious, valiant army of the planes!

Minna Irving

NOX MORTIS

The afternoon
Flutters and dies;
The fairy moon
Burns in the skies
As they grow darker, and the first stars shine
On night's rich mantle—purple like warm wine.

On each white road
Begins to crawl
The heavy Toad:
The night-birds call,
And round the trees the swift bats flit and wheel,
While from the barns the rats begin to steal.

So now must I
Bird of the night,
Toward the sky
Make wheeling flight,
And bear my poison o'er the gloomy land,
And let it loose with hard unsparing hand.

The chafers boom
With whirring wings,
And haunt the gloom
Which twilight brings—
So in nocturnal travel do I wail
As through the night the wingèd engines sail.

Death, Grief and Pain
Are what I give
O that the slain
Might live—might live!
I know them not, for I have blindly killed,
And nameless hearts with nameless sorrow filled.

Thrice cursèd War
Which bids that I
Such death should pour
Down from the sky.
O, Star of Peace, rise swiftly in the East
That from such slaying men may be released.

PAUL BEWSHER—*The Bombing of Bruges*

AEROPLANES

Do you roar to remind
Of what we know is there—
The threat now loud behind
Our singing summer air?

Do you fly low to warn
　　Of what will darken soon
Above our homes forlorn
　　The sun, the stars, the moon?—

Of what man-thought has made—
　　The wheels of loveless might
That never now are stayed,
　　Keep turning, day and night.

　　　　　ELIZABETH DARYUSH—*The Last Man*

THE SONG OF THE CRASHING WING

Higher than tinselled Heaven,
Lower than angels dare,
Loop to the fray, swoop on their prey,
The Killers of the Air.

We scorned the Galilean,
　　We mocked at Kingdom-Come:
The old Gods knew our paean—
　　Our dawn-loud engine hum:

The old red gods of slaughter,
　　The gods before the Jew!
We heard their cruel laughter,
　　Shrill round us, as we flew:

When, deaf to earth and pity,
　　Blind to the guns beneath,
We loosed upon the city
　　Our downward-plunging death.

The Sun-God watched our fighting;
　　No Christian priest could tame
Our deathly stuttered fighting:—
　　The whirled drum, spitting flame;

270

The roar of blades behind her;
  The banking plane up-tossed;
The swerve that sought to blind her;
  Masked faces, glimpsed and lost;

The joy-stick wrenched to guide her;
  The swift and saving zoom,
What time the shape beside her
  Went spinning to its doom.

No angel wings might follow
  Where, poised behind the fray,
We spied our Lord Apollo
  Stoop down to mark his prey—

The hidden counter-forces,
  The guns upon the road;
The tethered transport-horses,
  Stampeding, as we showed—

Dun hawks of death, loud-roaring—
  A moment to their eyes:
And slew; and pressed far-soaring;
  And dwindled up the skies.

But e'en Apollo's pinions
  Had faltered where we ran,
Low through his veiled dominions,
  To lead the charging van!

The tree-tops slathered under;
  The Red-Steel Killers knew,
Hard overhead, the thunder
  And backwash of her screw;

The blurred clouds raced above her;
  The blurred fields streaked below,

Where waited, crouched to cover,
  The foremost of our foe . . .

Banking, we saw his furrows
Leap at us, open wide:
Hell-raked the man-packed burrows;
  And crashed—and crashing, died.

    GILBERT FRANKAU—*The Judgment of Valhalla*

AN IRISH AIRMAN FORESEES HIS DEATH

I know that I shall meet my fate
Somewhere among the clouds above;
Those that I fight I do not hate,
Those that I guard I do not love;
My country is Kiltartan Cross,
My countrymen Kiltartan's poor;
No likely end could bring them loss
Or leave them happier than before.
Nor law, nor duty bade me fight,
Nor public men, nor cheering crowds,
A lonely impulse of delight
Drove to this tumult in the clouds;
I balanced all, brought all to mind,
The years to come seemed waste of breath,
A waste of breath the years behind,
In balance with this life, this death.

        W. B. YEATS

THE DAWN PATROL

Sometimes I fly at dawn above the sea,
Where, underneath, the restless waters flow—
  Silver, and cold, and slow.
Dim in the East there burns a new-born sun,

Whose rosy gleams along the ripples run,
    Save where the mist droops low,
Hiding the level loneliness from me.

And now appears beneath the milk-white haze
A little fleet of anchored ships, which lie
    In clustered company,
And seem as they are yet fast bound by sleep,
Although the day has long begun to peep,
    With red-inflamed eye,
Along the still, deserted ocean ways.
The fresh, cold wind of dawn blows on my face
As in the sun's raw heart I swiftly fly,
    And watch the seas glide by.
Scarce human seem I, moving through the skies,
And far removed from warlike enterprise—
    Like some great gull on high
Whose white and gleaming wings bear on through space.

Then do I feel with God quite, quite alone,
High in the virgin morn, so white and still,
    And free from human ill:
My prayers transcend my feeble earth-bound plaints—
As though I sang among the happy Saints
    With many a holy thrill—
As though the glowing sun were God's bright Throne.

My flight is done. I cross the line of foam
That breaks around a town of grey and red,
    Whose streets and squares lie dead
Beneath the silent dawn—then am I proud
That England's peace to guard I am allowed;
    Then bow my humble head,
In thanks to Him who brings me safely home.

PAUL BEWSHER

MISSING

'One of our seaplanes failed to return.'

(Admiralty Report, 22nd January 1918)

'La mer reprend le marin; le ciel reprend l'aviateur.'

Francy Lacroix

He hath gone hence: now therefore he is free
By grace of an invisible city,
Inheritor of a serener air,
Untouched by change or time, uncrazed by care.
He will not now return to those he knew,
He will not fly with those who gaily flew
Into the storm, into the cloud, into the night.
He has passed out upon the farthest flight
That ever airman ventures: on and on,
Beyond earthmark or airmark he has gone.
His seaplane, like a swimmer, clave the sea,
And, as she rose, shook off mortality;
Drawn into deeps of being, boundless tides
Of beauty, where no veil or bar divides
Body and spirit, shadow and the light,
Things that are seen and unseen, faith and sight.

E. Vine Hall—*In Full Flight*

THE GHOSTS OF THE EIGHTH ATTACK

When first the roar of a D.H.4
    Came sounding over the plain,
The clan who flew were tried and true,
    And sound of heart and brain,
Our Squadron then lost gallant men,
    And well we have learned their lack;
And we'll drink a toast to each brave ghost,—
    The Ghosts of the Eighth Attack.

Kingsland turned to a spin and burned,
　　Rex and Gallagher died
In battle flame on the field of fame,
　　With Mitchell by their side,
From Death unveiled they never quailed,
　　Or broke upon the rack,
But well we ken they fought like men,
　　The Ghosts of the Eighth Attack!

Dean and Bateman and Hollingsworth—
　　Death garnered, thigh and thew,
And Captain Shea, with his Irish way,—
　　Virgin and Hartmann too.
Robinson, Martin, Grodecki,
　　And Mackey, and Womack:
Brave hearts of gold that now lie cold,—
　　The Ghosts of the Eighth Attack

And I sometimes think, when the night winds howl,
　　And never a ship is out,
That I hear the roar of a D.H.4,
　　And the wail of wires in doubt;
And I think I see in a spectre ship
　　Spirits that *must* come back;
And I hail them then, who have died like *men*,—
　　The Ghosts of the Eighth Attack!

J. L. HITCHINGS

THE BALLAD OF THE BRISTOL FIGHTER

There's a good half-dozen buses
On which I've done a whack,
From the R.E.8 to the three-ton weight
Of the lumbering old Big Ack.

On a rotary-engined Avro,
I've attempted several tricks
And I'm quite a dab at steering a Crab
(Better known as a D.H.6.)

And many a first-rate joy-ride
Have I had on 'em last and first,
And many a strut have I had go phut,
And many a wheel tyre burst.
But none of them know the secret
Of making my heart rejoice
Like a well-rigged Bristol Fighter
With a two-six-four Rolls Royce.

She leans at her place on the tarmac
Like a tiger crouched for a spring,
From the arching spine of her fuselage line
To the ample spread of her wing.
With her tyres like sinews tautened
And her tail-skid's jaunty twist,
Her grey-cowled snout juts grimly out
Like a tight-clenched boxer's fist.

Is there a sweeter music,
A more contenting sound,
Than the purring clop of her broad-curved prop
As it gently ticks around?
Open her out crescendo
To a deep-toned swelling roar,
Till she quivers and rocks as she strains at the chocks
And clamours amain to soar,

Whisk 'em away, my hearties,
Taxi her into the wind,
Then away we skim on a spinning rim
With the tail well up behind;

Hold her down to a hundred,
Then up in a climbing turn
And off we sweep in a speckless sky
Till we catch our breath in the air Alp-high.
I wouldn't exchange my seat, not I,
For a thousand pounds to burn.

The Aeroplane

Songs they sang in the R.F.C., 1914-18

DEAD MUSICIANS

From you, Beethoven, Bach, Mozart,
  The substance of my dreams took fire.
You built cathedrals in my heart,
  And lit my pinnacled desire.
You were the ardour and the bright
  Procession of my thoughts towards prayer.
You were the wrath of storm, the light
  On distant citadels aflare.

Great names, I cannot find you now
  In these loud years of youth that strives
Through doom towards peace; upon my brow
  I wear a wreath of lives.
You have no part with lads that fought
  And laughed and suffered at my side.
Your fugues and symphonies have brought
  No memory of my friends that died.
For when my brain is on their track,
In slangy speech I call them back.
With fox-trot tunes their ghosts I charm.
'Another little drink won't do you any harm.'

> *I think of rag-time; a bit of rag-time;*
> *And see their faces crowding round*
> *To the sound of syncopated beat,*
> *They've got such jolly things to tell,*
> *Home from hell with a Blighty wound so neat...*

> . . . . .

And so the song breaks off; and I'm alone.
They're dead ... For God's sake stop that gramophone.

SIEGFRIED SASSOON

A MEMORY

We taxied out into position and took off in formation. Directly we got up we let out our aerials. We were wearing special flying-caps which had earphones fitted in them. Presently we heard H.'s high-pitched voice singing:

> 'Oh, there was a little hen, and she had a wooden leg,
> The best little hen that ever laid an egg,
> And she laid more eggs than any on the farm,
> And another little drink wouldn't do us any harm.
> Another little drink, another little drink—'

ROGER VEE—*Flying Minnows*

THE WRECK OF THE OLD F.E.

With apologies to the late lamented Schooner Hesperus

> It was an old F.E.2b,
>   That flew the wintry sky;
> The pilot had taken a second A.M.
>   To bear him company.

> Red were his eyes as the crimson rose,
>   His nose as the dawn of day;
> His feet as cold as the mess-room stove
>   As they ploughed their chilly way.

278

The skipper he sat in the pilot's seat,
   His heart was in his mouth,
As he watched how the veering wind did blow
   The clouds now west, now south.

Then up and spake the observer bold,
   With a gesture of his hand,
'I'm hanged if I know where the hell we are,
   So hurry up and land.'

'Last week the sky was full of planes,
   Today no planes we see.'
But the pilot spat on his aneroid,
   And a scornful laugh laughed he.

Higher and higher he climbed his bus,
   And looked for his escort bold;
But they were down in the mess-room hut
   (If you wish the truth to be told.)

Down came the storm and smote amain
   The F.E. in her strength;
She shuddered and stalled like a frightened steed,
   Then dropped a cable's length.

'Lie down, lie down, my little A.M.,
   And do not tremble so;
For I can weather the roughest gale
   That ever wind did blow.'

'Oh Captain! I hear a pop-pop-pop;
   Oh say, what may it be?'
'It's a blasted Hun on my blinking tail';
   And he turned around to see.

'Oh Captain! I see two crosses black;
   Oh say, what may it be?'
'Grab hold of that Lewis and shoot, you fool,
   And don't stand talking to me.'

'Oh Captain! I don't understand the gun,
    Oh say, what shall I do?'
But the Captain's words were wafted back,
    And broke the prop. in two.

Then down through the fleecy clouds below,
    The F.E. drifted fast;
The observer thought of his future,
    And the pilot thought of his past.

And ever the fitful gusts between
    A sound—what can it be?
'Twas Archie paying his last respects
    To the wreck of the old F.E.

The trenches were right beneath her bows,
    She drifted a weary wreck,
And the Captain swore if he DID get down,
    He'd break the blighter's neck.

She struck where the verdant waving grass
    Looked soft as a downy bed;
But a couple of cows got in her way,
    So she quietly stood on her head.

Full twenty yards across the ground
    The luckless pair were cast.
'I think I'll go,' said the second A.M.
    'The danger is not past.'

At daybreak in a barren field,
    He still was running round;
Whilst close behind the pilot came,
    Forever gaining ground.

The oil was frozen on his face,
    His mouth was full of sand,
But nearer came the avenger grim
    With the joystick in his hand.

Such was the wreck of the old F.E.
 In the land of rain and mud.
Lord, save us all from such an A.M.
 And make the weather dud.

OVER THE LINES

We were flying in formation and continued to keep our station,
 Though the wind was trying hard to sweep the sky.
And we watched the puffs of powder, heard the Archies
  booming louder
 And we didn't need to stop to reason why.
With the German lines below us, and a gale that seemed to
  throw us
 Into nowhere, as it would a schoolboy's kite,
We went skimming through the ether always keeping close
  together
 And we felt the joy of battle grip us tight.

Then from out of the horizon which we kept our eager eyes on
 Swept the Fokkers in their deadly fan-wise dash.
Soon the Vickers guns were cracking and a couple started
  backing,
 Whilst a third was sent down flaming in a flash.
How we blessed our Bristol Fighters as we closed in with the
  blighters,
 And we zoomed and banked and raced them through the air.

We abandoned our formation, but we won the situation,
 Won it easily, with four machines to spare.
Then Archie burst around us, and the beggar nearly found us,
 But we dived towards our lines without delay,
And we finished gay and merry from a binge of gin and sherry,
 For we knew we lived to see another day.

YOU'RE ONLY A P.B.O.

TUNE: *Bachelor Gay* from *The Maid of the Mountains*

When you get in the old machine to start on a damned O.P.
You cover yourself with tons of clothes and they're all of them
  N.B.G.,
  The pilot sits near the engine's warmth, his body with heat
    aglow,
Whilst you must stand in the back and cuss
Till the ice on your whiskers stalls the bus,
  You're only a P.B.O., yes, only a P.B.O.

CHORUS:
At seventeen he's shooting rather badly at a Pfaltz of tender
  blue,
At fifteen thou. you see him point out sadly some Huns of
  different hue,
  At ten or twelve he's shooting rather madly at six or eight or
    more.
When he fancies he is past hope
Fires a long burst as a last hope,
  And a Hun spins down on fire to the floor.

When you're doing an escort stunt and the Huns get on your
  tail,
You fire and aim till you see 'em flame and down they go like
  hail.
  Alas! the pilot's jealous scorn is a thing we learn to know.
You may get twenty Huns in flames,
Don't think they'll believe your claims,
  You're only a P.B.O.; yes, only a P.B.O.

CHORUS: At seventeen, etc.

282

We all of us know the case when the pilot came home alone,
No doubt it was only a slight mistake but his altitude's clearly
    shown,
    He suddenly shoved his joystick down as far as it would go,
'Hello, you seem to have gone?' he said,
'I fear you must be somewhat dead,
    But you're only a P.B.O., yes, only a P.B.O.'

CHORUS: At seventeen, etc.

When you're flying the old 'Nine A' on a bumpy, windy day,
And your engine begins to splutter out and you think you have
    lost your way,
    Be careful to keep your head to wind if you want to reduce
    your glide,
And side-slip over a down-wind fence,
If you want to remain inside your field,
    If you want to remain inside, you want to remain inside.

CHORUS: At seventeen, etc.

At eighty-five you head her in so nicely, a glide you should not
    exceed;
At seventy-five you flatten out precisely, and still you've got
    lots of speed.
    At sixty-five you pull the stick back gently and put her on the
    floor.
But at fifty you'll be stalling,
And you'll realize you're falling,
    And you'll crash her as she's never crashed before.

CHORUS: At seventeen, etc.

IN OTHER WORDS

I was fighting a Hun in the heyday of youth,
    Or perhaps 'twas a Nieuport or Spad.
I put in a burst at a moderate range
    And it didn't seem any too bad.
For he put down his nose in a curious way,
And as I watched him I am happy to say:

CHORUS: He descended with unparalleled rapidity,
        His velocity 't would beat me to compute.
    I speak with unimpeachable veracity,
        With evidence complete and absolute.
    He suffered from spontaneous combustion
        As towards terrestrial sanctuary he dashed,
    And underwent complete disintegration,
        In other words—he crashed!

I was telling the tale when a message came through
    To say 'twas a poor R.E.8
The news somewhat dashed me, I rather supposed
    I was in for a bit of a hate.
The C.O. approached me, I felt rather weak,
For his face went all mottled, and when he did speak:

CHORUS: He straffed me with unmitigated violence,
        With wholly reprehensible abuse.
    His language in its blasphemous simplicity
        Was rather more exotic than abstruse,
    He mentioned that the height of his ambition
        Was to see your humble servant duly hung.
    I returned to the Home Establishment next morning,
        In other words—I was stung.

As a pilot in France I flew over the lines
    And there met an Albatros Scout.

It seemed that he saw me, or so I presumed;
  His manoeuvre left small room for doubt.
For he sat on my tail without further delay
Of my subsequent actions I think I may say:

CHORUS: My turns approximated to the vertical,
          I deemed it most judicious to proceed.
        I frequently gyrated on my axis
          And attained colossal atmospheric speed,
        I descended with unparalleled momentum,
          My propeller's point of rupture I surpassed,
        And performed the most astounding evolutions,
          In other words, ——

I was testing a Camel on last Friday week,
  For the purpose of passing her out.
And before fifteen seconds of flight had elapsed
  I was filled with a horrible doubt,
As to whether intact I should land from my flight.
I half thought I'd crash—and I half thought quite right.

CHORUS: The machine it seemed to lack co-agulation,
          The struts and sockets didn't rendezvous,
        The wings had lost their super-imposition,
          Their stagger and their incidental, too!
        The fuselage developed undulations,
          The circumjacent fabric came unstitched,
        Instanter was reduction to components,
          In other words—she's pitched!

STORMY THE NIGHT

TUNE: *Asleep in the Deep*

Stormy the night and a lowering sky,
  Proudly the plane doth ride.

Hark how the passenger's startled cry
  Rings as he clutches the side.
There in his cockpit the pilot lays,
Cursing his ballast, who weakly prays.
Tho' death be near, he knows no fear,
For at his side are a dozen beer.

CHORUS: Brightly the flares from the landing ground blaze,
        Bidding us list to the hint it conveys.
          Pilot take care: Pilot take care.
        Hundreds have crashed, so beware, beware.
        Many brave hearts have neglected their charts,
          So beware, beware.

What of the tempest the following morn?
  There is no trace or sign,
Save where the wreckage bestrews the corn
  Peacefully the sun doth shine.
But ere the wild raging storm did stop
Two gallant airmen were caught on the hop,
No more to roam, afar from home,
No more forced landings because of the Gnôme.

CHORUS: Brightly flares from the landing ground blaze,
        Bidding us list to the hint it conveys.
          Pilot take care: Pilot take care.
        Hundreds have crashed, so beware, beware.
        Many brave hearts have been mixed with spare parts,
          So beware, beware.

A SQUADRON SONG

Twelve young pilots from (Squadron M),
Took the air one morn at eight,
They met fifty Huns, they say,
Over the middle of Tournai.

CHORUS: So early in the morning,
    So early in the morning,
    So early in the mor-r-r-ning,
    Before the break of day.

Hep was leading A Flight then,
(Murray) followed with B Flight men,
There were eight old Fokkers in the sun,
That is the way of the wily Hun.

CHORUS: So early in the morning, etc.

Hep got a Hun right on his tail,
He did a half-roll without fail,
Then his gun went dud they say,
So he came home and left the fray.

CHORUS: So early in the morning, etc.

A Flight followed back to the lines,
And there we met some D.H.9's,
They didn't see any Huns about,
Soon they went like a bloody scout.

CHORUS: So early in the morning, etc.

The wily Fokkers climbed aloft,
And thought ha! ha! here's something soft,
But we four Bristols came out of the sun,
And that soon stopped the beggars' fun.

CHORUS: So early in the morning, etc.

The P.B.O.s shot well that day,
And every gun got its Hun, they say,
(Trent) fired and kept them away,
While (Grant's) Very lights frightened them away.

CHORUS: So early in the morning, etc.

'Practically everyone who had taken part in the scrap had contributed some verses to this epic. . . . No-one knew all the verses, but each man knew some of them, and the solo was carried on by different members as the song progressed. But at the end of each verse we all roared out the chorus with vast enjoyment.'

ROGER VEE—*Flying Minnows*

SONG BOOKS OF THE WAR

In fifty years, when peace outshines
Remembrance of the battle lines,
Adventurous lads will sigh and cast
Proud looks upon the plundered past.
On summer's morn or winter's night,
Their hearts will kindle for the fight,
Reading a snatch of soldier-song,
Savage and jaunty, fierce and strong;
And through the angry marching rhymes
Of blind regret and haggard mirth,
They'll envy us the dazzling times
When sacrifice absolved our earth.

Some ancient man with silver locks
Will lift his weary face to say:
'War was a fiend who stopped our clocks
Although we met him grim and gay.'
And then he'll speak of Haig's last drive,
Marvelling that any came alive
Out of the shambles that men built
And smashed, to cleanse the world of guilt.
But the boys will grin and side-long glance
Will think, 'Poor Grandad's day is done.'
And dream of lads who fought in France
And lived in time to share the fun.

SIEGFRIED SASSOON

XII
Dunkirk and
The Battle of Britain
1940

A YOUNG ENGLISH AIRMAN

O smiling, sun-burned youth who rode the sky
Like to the sparrow-hawk or summer swift,
And watched your shadow flitting on the drift
Far underneath you as you hurried by,

Six months ago today you put off bird
To gleam as ion in a nation's will,
To save the ruined friends and then lie still,
Spring never to be touched by summer's word.

Often unseen by those you helped to save
You rode the air above that foreign dune
And died like the unutterably brave
That so your friends might see the English June.

Haply, in some sharp instant in mid-sky,
When you, at the bird's summit, took the lunge
Of the foe's bitterness that made you die,
And the bright bird declined into her plunge,

You, from the Heaven, saw, in English chalk
White, about Dover, some familiar track,
That feet of yours would never again walk
Since you were killed and never coming back,

Yet knew, that your young life, as price paid over
Let thousands live to tread that track to Dover.

JOHN MASEFIELD—The Nine Days' Wonder

THE BATTLE OF BRITAIN, 1940
The Royal Air Force

Never in the field of human conflict was so much owed by so
many to so few.   WINSTON CHURCHILL

BETWEEN MIDNIGHT AND MORNING

You that have faith to look with fearless eyes
　　Beyond the tragedy of a world at strife,
And trust that out of night and death shall rise
　　The dawn of ampler life;

Rejoice, whatever anguish rend your heart,
　　That God has given you, for a priceless dower,
To live in these great times and have your part
　　In Freedom's crowning hour.

That you may tell your sons who see the light
　　High in the Heaven, their heritage to take:—
'I saw the powers of darkness put to flight!
　　I saw the morning break!'

OWEN SEAMAN

Who are these that fly as a cloud
And as the doves to their windows?
Surely the Isles shall wait for me
And the ships of Tarshish first,
To bring thy sons from far
Their silver and gold with them.

ISAIAH

AIRMEN FROM OVERSEAS

Who are these that come from the ends of the oceans,
Coming as the swallows come out of the South
In the glory of Spring? They are come among us
With purpose in the eyes, with a smile on the mouth.

These are they who have left the familiar faces,
Sights, sounds and scents of familiar land,
Taking no care for security promised aforetime,
Sweetness of home and the future hope had planned.

A lode-star has drawn them; Britain, standing alone
Clear in the darkness, not to be overcome,
Though the huge masses of hate are hurled against her,
Wherever the spirit of freedom breathes, is Home.

Soon are they joined with incomparable comrades.
Britain's flower and Britain's pride,
Against all odds, despising the boastful Terror,
On joyous wings in the ways of the wind they ride.

From afar they battle for our ancient island,
Soaring and pouncing, masters of the skies.
They are heard in the night by the lands betrayed and captive,
And a throbbing of hope to their thunder-throb replies.

To dare incredible things, from the ends of ocean
They are coming and coming, over the perilous seas.
How shall we hail them? Truly there are no words
And no song worthy of these.

LAURENCE BINYON

YOUTH IN THE SKIES

Those who were children yesterday
Now move in lovely flight,
Swift-glancing as the shooting stars
That cleave the summer night;

A moment flashed, they came and went,
Horizons rise and fall,
The speed of valour lifts them up
And strength obeys their call.

The downs below are breathing peace
With thyme and butterflies,
And sheep at pasture in the shade—
And now from English skies

Those who were children yesterday
Look down with other eyes:
Man's desperate folly was not theirs
But theirs the sacrifice.

Old men may wage a war of words,
Another race are these,
Who flash to glory dawn and night
Above the starry seas.

HERBERT ASQUITH—*Youth in the Skies*

OCTOBER 1940

When leaves like guineas start to fall
And sycamore and elm begin
Red tears to shed, then autumn's in
And summer gone beyond recall.

Thick, thick they fell from London trees
In years that seem an age ago;
How cantered they down Rotten Row
And ran down Broad Walk with the breeze!

The children laughed to see them run
And caught them in their merry flight,
And we were glad for their delight
Beneath the thin October sun.

But there's another fall today,
When bombs instead of leaves come down
To drive our children out of Town
And us to ground. We will repay.

Punch

LONDON, 1940

Beloved London's ancient walls,
   Battered by hail of steel and fire,
   Look down with proud and scornful ire
On all the ruin of its halls.

So with disdain the pillared rock,
   Deep rooted in mid ocean's bed,.
   Undaunted proudly lifts its head
Scorning the waves' imperious shock.

So too the oak, that bows before
   The furious raging of the blast,
   The tyranny now overpast,
Unconquered rears itself once more.

In vain upon our stricken lands
   The flying hordes rain death and fear:
   Fighting for all we hold most dear
Old London's spirit firmly stands.

A. A. MILNE

NIGHT BOMBERS

Eastward they climb, black shapes against the grey
Of falling dusk, gone with the nodding day
From English fields.
               Not theirs the sudden glow
Of triumph that their fighter-brothers know;
Only to fly through cloud, through storm, through night
Unerring, and to keep their purpose bright,
Nor turn until, their dreadful duty done,
Westward they climb to race the awakened sun.

Punch

APOCALYPSE, 1940

Urgent, doom-heralding, the first wild wail
Wells out upon the tense and listening air,
Grim preface to the thunder and the flare
Of warring earth and sky. To what avail?
For no averting knows that falling flail
Whose cruel Fury-shaken lash heaps high
(Strange winnowing!) the chaff that's used to fly
As now the grain flies to rich barns, and pale
Souls, man-tormented, meet their Master's smile.

In world-wreck and in iron hurricane
Dim eyes grow keen again and halt words winged,
And though no lamp shines or law limits trial
Our life's not friendless nor our death in vain,
By one Light lighted and by one Love ringed.

A. B. 3.

THE FLYING INSTRUCTOR'S LAMENT

'What did you do in the war, Daddy?
How did you help us to win?'
'Circuits and bumps and turns, laddy,
And how to get out of a spin.'

Woe and alack and misery me! I trundle around in the sky,
And instead of machine-gunning Nazis I'm teaching young
    hopefuls to fly;
Thus is my service rewarded, my years of experience paid,
Never a Hun have I followed right down nor ever gone out on a
    raid.

They don't even let us go crazy, we have to be safe and sedate,
So it's nix on inverted approaches, they stir up the C.F.I.'s
hate.
For it's oh! such a naughty example, and what will the A.O.C.
think!
But we never get posted to fighters—we just get a spell on the
Link.

So it's circuits and bumps from morning till noon, and instru-
ment-flying till tea.
'Hold her off, give her bank, put your undercart down, you're
skidding, you're slipping'—that's me.
And as soon as you've finished with one course, like a flash up
another one bobs,
And there's four more to show round the cockpit and four more
to try out the knobs.

But sometimes we read in the papers of the deeds that old
pupils have done,
And we're proud to have seen their beginnings and shown them
the way to the sun;
So if *you* find the money and turn out the planes *we*'ll give all we
know to the men
Till they cluster the sky with their triumphs and burn out the
Beast from his den.

Punch

A MESSAGE TO THE AIR DEFENCE
CADET CORPS

The pilot's combat reports are kept in the archives of the Air
Ministry. Sometimes the writing seems tired. Sometimes they
are in scratchy pencil. They tell the story of the war in the air
in modest words—they are just facts, set down by men who are
too grand to use adjectives in describing their deeds.

CAPT. BALFOUR, M.P., Under-Secretary of State for Air

FAREWELL TO FEAR

The following lines were written by an airman after a recent crash.

Three days ago
Eternity stood nigh me,
    Clean, white as snow
With nothing to deny me
    A passing mild,
Some little fame behind me
    For wife and child
Before dull age could blind me.

    Senseless I lie,
Five hours unconscious witness,
    To live or die?
Nature's stern test of fitness.
    Of life the gift
Again so strangely given,
    Gladly I lift
By some new strength reshriven.

    Farewell to fear,
The doubts that ever tied me,
    The road is clear
With England's need to guide me.
    So high the quest
That every qualm is treason;
    Life at its best
Is Faith beyond all reason.

The Times

THERE IS NO SANCTUARY FOR BRAVE MEN

There is no sanctuary for brave men,
　　Danger allures them as it were a sun;
What they have dared they will dare once again
　　And so continue till the day is done.

There is no satiation of brave deeds,
　　One draws another as wit calls on wit.
Oh, what a soul it is that ever heeds
　　The hour's necessity and springs to it!

There's no intimidation of great thought,
　　Knowledge attracts it as the heavens the eye;
Though dangerous 'tis to learn, it will be taught,
　　Pushing its question to the uttermost Why.

There is no sanctuary for brave men,
　　Dangers allure them as the moon the tide;
What they have dared they will dare once again
　　Though they lose all else in the world beside.

　　　　　　　　　　　　　　　　　Punch

AN AIRMAN TO HIS MOTHER

Dearest Mother,—Though I feel no premonition at all, events are moving rapidly, and I have instructed that this letter be forwarded to you should I fail to return from one of the raids which we shall shortly be called upon to undertake. You must hope on for a month, but at the end of that time you must accept the fact that I have handed my task over to the extremely capable hands of my comrades of the Royal Air Force, as so many splendid fellows have already done.

First, it will comfort you to know that my role in this war has been of the greatest importance. Our patrols far out over the North Sea have helped to keep the trade routes clear for our convoys and supply ships, and on one occasion our information was instrumental in saving the lives of the men in a crippled lighthouse relief ship. Though it will be difficult for you, you will disappoint me if you do not at least try to accept the facts dispassionately, for I shall have done my duty to the utmost of my ability. No man can do more, and no one calling himself a man could do less.

I have always admired your amazing courage in the face of continual setbacks; in the way you have given me as good an education and background as anyone in the country; and always kept up appearances without ever losing faith in the future. My death would not mean that your struggle has been in vain. Far from it. It means that your sacrifice is as great as mine. Those who serve England must expect nothing from her; we debase ourselves if we regard our country as merely a place in which to eat and sleep.

History resounds with illustrious names who have given all, yet their sacrifice has resulted in the British Empire, where there is a measure of peace, justice, and freedom for all, and where a higher standard of civilization has evolved, and is still evolving, than anywhere else. But this is not only concerning our own land. Today we are faced with the greatest organized challenge to Christianity and civilization that the world has ever seen, and I count myself lucky and honoured to be the right age and fully trained to throw my full weight into the scale. For this I have to thank you. Yet there is more work for you to do. The home front will still have to stand united for years after the war is won. For all that can be said against it, I still maintain that this war is a very good thing; every individual is having the chance to give and dare all for his principle like the martyrs of old. However long the time may be, one thing can never be altered—I shall have lived and died an Englishman. Nothing else matters one jot nor can anything ever change it.

You must not grieve for me, for if you really believe in religion and all that it entails that would be hypocrisy. I have no fear of death; only a queer elation. . . . I would have it no other way. The universe is so vast and so ageless that the life of one man can only be justified by the measure of his sacrifice. We are sent to this world to acquire a personality and a character to take with us that can never be taken from us. Those who just eat and sleep, prosper and procreate, are no better than animals if all their lives they are at peace.

I firmly and absolutely believe that evil things are sent into the world to try us; they are sent deliberately by our Creator to test our metal because He knows what is good for us. The Bible is full of cases where the easy way out has been discarded for moral principles.

I count myself fortunate in that I have seen the whole country and known men of every calling. But with the final test of war I consider my character fully developed. Thus at my early age my earthly mission is already fulfilled and I am prepared to die with just one regret, and one only—that I could not devote myself to making your declining years more happy by being with you; but you will live in peace and freedom and I shall have directly contributed to that, so here again my life will not have been in vain.

Your loving Son,

_____

XIII
Wings of Peace

A VERSE

O! that I had wings like a dove, for then would I fly away, and
   be at rest.
Lo, then would I wander far off, and remain in the wilderness.
I would hasten my escape from the windy storm and tempest.

THE PSALMIST

THE FREEMASONRY OF THE AIR

Nor must you forget that lure of flying, the 'Freemasonry of
the Air'. Even during the war the sporting instinct that existed
between two opposing Flying Forces was proved time out of
number by acts of courtesy and respect paid by each side to the
enemy's fallen. Today it is possible when flying round Europe,
to land on an aerodrome, and on entering a pilots' mess, to sit
down with pilots of half a dozen nationalities. I can call to mind
an occasion when I dined at Brussels with two Russians, one
German, two Frenchmen, a Belgian, two Swedes, a Dane and
two Englishmen. The gathering was certainly international;
but first and foremost it was aviational. All these men were
united by the same great bond. National differences were swept
aside. Their banner was the banner of Aviation.

ALAN COBHAM—Skyways

THE AVIATOR'S WORLD

The aviator lives in a world a little different from that of the
ordinary man in the street. He has a different idea and range of
conception of the earth he dwells upon, for by means of aviation we are going to learn more about geography than by any
other development in history. The speed of flying will make us
realize how small the world is and how petty are our quarrels,

for aviation cares nought for frontiers, and by this quickened means of transport the races of the earth will have greater intercourse with, and knowledge of each other.

ALAN COBHAM—*Skyways*

INITIATION

That I have lived to see men fly
In remote reaches of the sky,
Ready the darkest hour to dare
In the deep spaces of the air,
To take their station by the stars,
And to stand sentry at the bars
Of sunset: to excel in speed
The very vulture, to exceed
For height the hawk, for grace the gull,
Man's marks and limits to annul,
Till earth shrink to an island, hung
The heaven's other orbs among,
And the world but a shadow seems
Of unintelligible dreams,
Staggers my soul. Therefore I see,
As knit in one society,
Seers, saints and airmen; all who rise
To the pure place of the clear skies
And read, as in a mirror's face,
The hidden things of time and space.

E. VINE HALL—*In Full Flight*

IN THE COCKPIT

Nor is there a more ideal place in the world for meditation than the cockpit of a 'plane as you race across the sky at 70 or 100 miles an hour. If the air is clear and you are high enough from the earth not to be interested in its affairs, and if your motor is singing a melody of power that is one long rhythmical harmony, you and your 'plane seem to merge into one. The swiftness of your flight seems to blow the cobwebs from your brain, and you can do more clear thinking in two hours there than you can do in two days in a crowded city.

E. NELSON—*The First World Flight*

AVIATION AND PEACE

The advance of scientific knowledge has not been accompanied by a corresponding development in the realm of ethics and more knowledge of the human mind and its behaviour is needed. Man's knowledge—and thus control—of himself is fundamental to the proper use of the aeroplane as it is to the use of the motor car.

It is apparent from the history of aeronautics that the engineers and technical experts who actually developed the aeroplane were not concerned with the moral or political results of their work; on the other hand, men such as Cayley appear at least to have realized the social and economic implications. The function of the engineer is to apply the co-ordinated knowledge of the man of science and the accumulated experience of ages to the increase of the amenities of human life. His contact with humanity should thus be closer than that of the research worker in pure science and it is logical that we should look to him for some control of the instruments which he has created. Therein, it is suggested, lies the only immediate hope for the proper application of scientific inventions—and in particular the aeroplane—to the enrichment of human life.

It has been seen that, since the invention of the aeroplane, aviation has grown very rapidly; but there is apparently no corresponding advance in friendly intercourse between peoples, or any indication of a beneficial influence in that sense, and relations become more and not less strained, due, in part at any rate, to the fear of devastation which air power brings in its train. The world expenditure on offensive and defensive air power now probably exceeds four hundred million pounds annually [1] and this expenditure does not result in any universal feeling of security—rather the reverse, since in any future conflict the civil populations are likely to suffer in a manner hitherto unknown.

It is necessary to consider these factors if one considers flight at all. They concern the man of science, the aircraft engineer, and the air-pilot—in fact all who are occupied in the creation, construction and use of aircraft—as much as the ordinary citizen. No-one can wholly escape responsibility, but those who are engaged in the world-wide science and calling of aviation should be in a better position to influence and to exercise that measure of control which is essential if the machine is not ultimately to destroy the mind that made it. Man's reaction to the changes which the advance in exact knowledge and its application have brought about—so aptly described as 'the impact of science upon society'—is the basic consideration. A new technique is required to meet the changed conditions—in this case the condition resulting from the introduction of a new and potent weapon—and it may well consist in a reconstruction of authority, so that, in the realm of scientific attainment, control of such inventions as may constitute a great benefit or a threat to society will be vested in some international body.

In the specific case we are now considering—which is such a glaring example of human failure—the principle may prove feasible since there exists an increasing community of spirit among airmen and technicians of all nationalities which may one day exercise a profound influence. A more active co-operation between those learned societies and other organisations, whose declared purpose is to disseminate knowledge and further the cause of flight throughout the world, may also

[1] 1937.

prove beneficial. It is significant that the identity of purpose which in the past has been a characteristic of workers in scientific research is now extending to those who operate the machines, and in particular to those who fly. The tendency is one which should be carefully fostered because, in the fullness of time, it may render the aeroplane the most effective of all instruments for promoting and maintaining world peace.

Meanwhile we cannot do other than revert to the interpretation of the history of human flight—the historic background which may influence to some extent the behaviour of future generations of airmen. We find that the honours are fairly equally divided. In Italy the Renaissance produced the reasoned speculations of Leonardo da Vinci and Francesco de Lana; France produced the balloon and the first airship; in England Sir George Cayley defined the aeroplane, and in Germany Otto Lilienthal experimented in the air and the internal combustion engine was born; America produced the Wright brothers and the first successful aeroplane, while from Spain came the invention of the autogiro and from Russia the inspiration of mass air-mindedness.

Is it too much to hope that this world-wide division of responsibility for the development of human life may lead ultimately to a like sharing of the responsibility of its use?

M. J. B. DAVY—*Interpretive History of Flight*

A MESSAGE TO THE AIR DEFENCE CADET CORPS

You will take on wings and write another story of courage across the English skies. I hope with all my heart that it will be a story of peace; that you will become the pilots who will mark out new air routes in the world, carry merchandise to isolated countries, passengers across the seas, and help and medical aid to those who live in the back blocks of new countries. I hope

that peace will come soon enough to allow you to be the great
pilots of the new age, when one of man's greatest inventions
will be used, not for his destruction, but for his good, his
enlightenment, and his prosperity.

Captain Harold Balfour, M.P., Under-Secretary of State
for Air

LIGHT

Break out, O lives of wonderment, that drive
The chariot-steeds of Nature! Break away
Into a world-dominion of the mind
As new as your machines! Your courses rise
Upon the pathway of the winds that blow,
Unchecked, across the long-divided shores
And range above the cloud-realms: you can speak
To unseen millions in their silent homes
Throughout the listening world: your tones are heard
Across Atlantic, and the barriers fall
Of time and place. The trail of yesterday,
So newly blazed into the secret wood
Of Nature's marvels, is today a road
Trodden by children in the simple faith
Of Life's acceptance, and tomorrow calls
As a magician throned amid the stars.
Nothing is now impossible: mankind
Stands kingly on the stubborn elements
And over Earth a unity is made.

A unity of scientific truth,
A unity of moment and of sound—
How much is left of jewels limitless
In the region of man's mind! How much still is
That overburdened man before the dawn

Of these great conquests! As your goal is truth
In all things to your knowledge provable—
As grain by grain the mountain of man's power
Is lifted through the universe, take heed
Of other, older truth. Earth's unity
Is still a discord, though man's life be rich
In daily easement of new majesties.
Ungrateful for the monarchy of mind
That covers Earth with huddled multitudes,
Man counts himself but little happier made
Than when its youth was wild and ignorant.
New barriers rise to take the place of old:
If time and place be free, man still is chained
To evils old and evils newly sprung
Out of the roots of freedom, and the load
Seems greater to his conscious, quickened mind.
Earth's peoples hum in massed monotony;
The craftsman's shadow haunts the great machine.
The tree of knowledge flowers, and yet its fruit,
Unsweetened, is but bitter—discontents
Within them have co-equal power of growth
With the new dominion over Nature's bounds,
Save wisdom, guiding knowledge, tend the soil.

Changes and wonders, a nda thousand miles
Raising to us a barrier less than five
To our forefathers! Are we therefore won
To greater understanding of the needs
That prey, unchanged, upon the human heart?
Are nations grown more brotherly, with war
Become a thought of horror? Man has found
A hundred ways of beating back disease
From widened life, but he has also found
A hundred ways of dealing wider death

311

And gropes about the finding, hesitant,
Thinking in terms of the old unhappiness
And longing for a future without fear.

Out and away, O lives of wonderment,
We need to burst; out of the circle grim
That holds the human spirit we must rise,
Not by the bending of our minds alone
To truths of science and the icy probe,
But on our pulses, all our senses tuned
To the songs and dirges of humanity.
New light is streaming on us through our minds,
Linking the altered world: let it be light,
The light of truth and love—and love is truth—
Illumining the heart from home to home,
From land to land, till unity be real,
Till thought, unshackled in a world of change,
Adventurous journeys to the heights of man
And greets the sunrise of felicity.

LORD GORELL—*Unheard Melodies*

IN THE FUTURE

The age of speed, whether at night in a fast car, or in an aeroplane breasting a storm, life has won a new magic, magic that will grow stronger as the age advances. What regions of ether will a man leave unknown? As he is lifted above the rainbow or sees the blue sparks where the thunderstorms are forged and hears the hammers in his ears, the whole universe sprawls at his feet and he is the god he thought he was. What are the stars but the lights of more cities at the end of roads? And the clouds but the meadows of another world? And then when the other gods hurl thunderbolts afire all round, gleaming and echoing more savagely than shells, and he twists, falls between the jagged flashes and drops like a plummet so many miles to his own still earth, there is no fear in that death, because in the wild light he has glimpsed his own divinity.

The age of speed grows, men have taken wings and no bounds can be set to their audacity, their desire cannot be curbed to cleave the very dome of heaven and see what waits beyond. . . . This is what the new era, so little now, so immense of promise, will achieve for us when the universe becomes our world and we swear once again, at length, in a Divine, not a simian origin; and who would not so swear, who lying on the clouds as on a couch, near the thunder in the winds, or gazing down upon the lights of many worlds and planets like the spilt diamonds of a necklace, would believe the clay that moulded him to have been quarried on any other mountain than Olympus?

MICHAEL BURN—*Wheels take Wings*

CHORUS FROM PROMETHEUS UNBOUND

Whence come ye, so wild and so fleet,
For sandals of lightning are on your feet,
And your wings are soft and swift as thought,
And your eyes are as love which is veilèd not?

We come from the mind
Of human kind
Which was late so dusk, and obscene, and blind,
Now 'tis an ocean
Of clear emotion,
A heaven of serene and mighty motion.

From that deep abyss
Of wonder and bliss,
Whose caverns are crystal palaces;
From those skiey towers,
Where Thought's crowned powers
Sit watching your dance, ye happy Hours!

From the dim recesses
Of woven caresses,
Where lovers catch ye by your loose tresses
From the azure isles,
Where sweet Wisdom smiles,
Delaying your ships with her siren wiles.

From the temples high
Of Man's ear and eye,
Roofed over Sculpture and Poesy;
From the murmurings
Of the unsealed springs
Where Science bedews her Daedal wings.

Years after years,
Through blood and tears,
And a thick hell of hatreds, and hopes, and fears;
We waded and flew,
And the islets were few
Where the bud-blighted flowers of happiness grew.

Our feet now, every palm,
Are sandalled with calm,
And the dew of our wings is a rain of balm;
And, beyond our eyes,
The human love lies
Which makes all it gazes on Paradise.

Our spoil is won,
Our task is done,
We are free to dive, or soar, or run;
Beyond and around,
Or within the bound
Which clips the world with darkness round.

We'll pass the eyes
Of the starry skies
Into the hoar deep to colonize:
Death, Chaos, and Night,
From the sound of our flight,
Shall flee, like mist from a tempest's might.

And Earth, Air, and Light,
And the Spirit of Might,
Which drives round the stars in their fiery flight;
And Love, Thought and Breath,
The powers that quell Death,
Wherever we soar shall assemble beneath.

And our singing shall build
In the void's loose field
A world for the Spirit of Wisdom to wield;
We will take our plan
From the new world of man,
And our work shall be called the Promethean.

P. B. SHELLEY

INDEX OF AUTHORS

ACKNOWLEDGEMENTS

The Editor and the Publishers wish to thank the authors or their representatives for permission to use extracts from their works. They also wish to thank the following for permission to reprint copyright material:—

Messrs. George Allen and Unwin and the author for the extract from P. E. Cleator (*Rockets Through Space*); Messrs. Ernest Benn and the authors for the poem by Eden Phillpotts (*100 Lyrics*) and the poem by John Oxenham (*Selected Poems*); Messrs. Basil Blackwell and Mott and the authors or their representatives for the extract from J. Laughton Fielding (*Daedalus*) and the poem by Humbert Wolfe (*Early Poems*); Messrs. William Blackwood and the author for the poem by Alfred Noyes (*The Collected Poems of Alfred Noyes*); Messrs. Jonathan Cape and the authors for the poem by W. H. Davies (*Collected Poems*), the poem by Robert Frost (*A Further*

317

Range), the poem by Michael Roberts (*Elegy for the Fallen Climbers*) and the poems by Cecil Day Lewis (*Overtures To Death*); Messrs. W. and R. Chambers for the extract from Amy Johnson (*Skyroads of the World*); Messrs. Chapman and Hall and the author for the extracts from Ivor B. Hart (*The Mechanical Investigations of Leonardo da Vinci*); Messrs. Chatto and Windus and the authors for the poems by Gilbert Frankau (*City of Fear and Other Poems* and *The Judgment of Valhalla*) and for the extract from David Garnett (*A Rabbit in the Air*); Messrs. William Collins and the author for the extracts from E. C. Vivian (*A History of Aeronautics*). Messrs. Doubleday Doran and Company and the Aero Club of America for the extracts from *Navigating the Air*; Messrs. A. F. Denny and Mrs. Vine Hall for the poems by E. Vine Hall (*In Full Flight*); Messrs. Gerald Duckworth and the authors for the extracts from E. McCurdy (*Leonardo da Vinci's Note Books*) and for the extract from F. D. Tredrey (*Pilot's Summer*); Messrs. Erskine Macdonald and author for the poems by Paul Bewsher (*The Dawn Patrol*); Messrs. Farrar and Rinehart and the author for the extracts from John Williams Andrews (*Prelude to Icaros*); Messrs. G. T. Foulis and the author for the extract from Michael Burn (*Wheels Take Wings*); Messrs. Victor Gollancz and the author for the poem by Fredegond Shove (*New English Poems*); Messrs. William Heinemann and the authors or their representatives for the poem by the Hon. Maurice Baring (*Collected Poems*), for the poem by John Masefield (*Collected Poems of John Masefield*), reprinted by permission of the author, for the extract from A. de Saint Exupéry (*Wind, Sand, Stars*), and for the poems by Siegfried Sassoon (*Selected Poems* and *Counterattack and Other Poems*); Messrs. George Harrap and the author for the poem from G. P. Putnam (*Last Flight*); Messrs. Hodder and Stoughton and the authors or their representatives for the poems by Paul Bewsher (*The Bombing of Bruges*) and for the extract from the late Lord Birkenhead (*The World in 2030*); Messrs. William Hodge and the authors for the extracts from the Marquis of Clydesdale and Flt. Lt. D. F. McIntyre (*The Pilots' Book of Everest*);

Acknowledgements

The Hogarth Press and the author for the poem by Cecil Day Lewis (*A Time to Dance*); Messrs. Hutchinson and the author for the extracts from Lowell Thomas (*The First World Flight*); Messrs. Michael Joseph for the extract from Filson Young (*Growing Wings*); Messrs. John Lane and Air Commodore Fellowes and other members of the Flight for extracts from *First Over Everest*; Messrs. Longmans Green for the extracts from Otto Lilienthal (*Birdflight as the Basis of Aviation*); Messrs. Longmans Green of New York and the author for the poem by C. L. O'Donnell (*The Rime of the Rood*); Messrs. Macmillan and the author for the poems by Laurence Binyon (*Sirens* and *Airmen from Overseas*); Messrs. Macmillan and Mrs. W. B. Yeats for the poem by W. B. Yeats (*Selected Poems*); the Macmillan Company, New York, and the author for the poem by R. P. Tristram Coffin (*Collected Poems*); Messrs. Methuen and the author for the extract from Gertrude Bacon (*Memories of Land and Sky*); Messrs. John Murray for the poems by Lord Gorell (*Many Mansions* and *Unheard Melodies*); the Oxford University Press and the authors for the poems by Elizabeth Daryush (*The Last Man*) and the poems by W. J. Turner (*Selected Poems*); Messrs. Putnam and the author for the extract from Rear-Admiral R. E. Byrd (*Antarctic Discovery*); Messrs. Rich and Cowan and the author for the extract from K. C. Gandar Dower (*Amateur Adventure*); Messrs. George Routledge and the author for the extracts from Jean Cocteau (*Round the World Again in Eighty Days*); Messrs. Sampson, Low, Marston and Company and the authors for the extracts from H. Mignet (*The Flying Flea*) and for extracts from C. C. Turner (*Old Flying Days*); Messrs. Charles Scribner's Sons for the poem by Duncan Campbell Scott (*Scribner's Magazine*); Messrs. Sidgwick and Jackson and the authors or their representatives for the poem by H. Asquith (*Youth in the Skies*) and for the poems by Jeffery Day (*Poems and Rhymes*); His Majesty's Stationery Office and the author for the extract from M. J. B. Davey (*The Interpretive History of Flight* (Science Museum)); the Western Society of Engineers for the extract from a lecture by Wilbur Wright; Dr. Griffith Brewer and the Royal Aeronautical Society for the extract from the Wilbur Wright Memorial Lecture; the Rt. Hon. Winston Churchill for extracts from a speech—19th July 1909; Miss G. M. Bacon for the extract from J. M. Bacon (*Dominion of the Air*); A. A. Milne for his poem, *London 1940*; Laurence Housman for his poems from *The Heart of Peace*; T. W. Ramsey for his poem from *Four Witchballs*; H. G. Wells for extracts from *The War in the Air* and *A Year of Prophesying*; Air Commodore MacNeece Foster for the poems 'An Airman's Te Deum' and 'Laus Deo in Excelsis'; *The Aeroplane* for verses by J. O. P. E. (1922) and 'The Ballad of the Bristol Fighter' (1918); the *Atlantic Monthly* for the poem by Dr. George E. Woodberry; the *Daily Mail* for extracts from articles on *The First Cross-Channel Flight*; the *Dublin Magazine* for the poem by Michael Scot; *The Month* for 'Apocalypse 1940'; the *News Chronicle* for the extract from the *Daily News*, 26th July 1909; the *New York Sun* for the poem by Minna Irving; the *Poetry Review* for 'Night Rides with the Mail Plane', 'The Light on Bolling Field', 'The Night Mail', 'Flight', 'Byrd—Explorer', 'Unsung', 'Flight', 'Wreck of the Uiver', 'Ghosts of the Eighth Attack' and 'To an Aviator'; *Poetry* (U.S.A.) and the author for the poem by Harold Rosenberg, 'Voyage to the End of Night'; *Popular Flying* for 'Songs they sang in the R.F.C.' and for 'Aviator—aged 6'; the Proprietors of *Punch* for 'Flying Machines', 'This is the Hour', 'There is no Sanctuary for Brave Men', 'October 1940', 'Night Bombers', 'To a Favourite Barrage Balloon', 'The Flying Instructor's Lament', and the poem by the late Sir Owen Seaman, 'Between Midnight and Morning'; the *Spectator* for the extract, 'The Zeppelin Aerial Machine'; *The Times* for 'An Airman's Letter to his Mother', 'A Climb in a Cloud', 'Airmen who do not Fly', 'Pilots of the New Age', 'Farewell to Fear', 'London 1940', and 'Youth in the Skies'. The Editor and Publishers regret that due to wartime circumstances they have been unable to get in touch with one or two authors and they have assumed their consent.